HARDPRESS.NET
HOME OF HARD-TO-FIND BOOKS

Questions on the Orders for Morning and Evening Prayer, and on the Litany, by I.F.
by Isabel Francis

Address:
HardPress
8345 NW 66TH ST #2561
MIAMI FL 33166-2626
USA
Email: info@hardpress.net

600097507Y

QUESTIONS

ON THE

Orders for Morning and Evening Prayer,

And on the Litany.

BY I. F.,

AUTHOR OF "A SIMPLE EXPLANATION OF THE CHURCH CATECHISM."

Published under the Direction of the Tract Committee.

LONDON:

SOCIETY FOR PROMOTING CHRISTIAN KNOWLEDGE.

SOLD AT THE DEPOSITORIES:

77, GREAT QUEEN STREET, LINCOLN'S-INN FIELDS;

4, ROYAL EXCHANGE; 48, PICCADILLY;

AND BY ALL BOOKSELLERS.

TABLE OF CONTENTS.

———◦◆◦———

QUESTIONS

ON THE

Orders for Morning & Evening Prayer and on the Litany.

———•◦•———

THE PRAYER-BOOK.

INTRODUCTION.—PART I. PUBLIC WORSHIP.

What is this book called?—The Prayer-book.

Find the first page.   What is it called there?
—The " Book of Common Prayer."

What does "Common Prayer" mean?—Prayer
for all Christians to use together.

When do we use the Prayer-book?—When we
go to church.

What do we go to church for?—To worship
God together.

What is that worship called?—Public worship.

Are we ever told in the Bible that we ought
to worship God in His house?—Yes, very often.

Can you repeat a verse about it?—" O go your
way into His gates with thanksgiving, and into
His courts with praise."   Psalm c. 3 (Prayer-
book version).

I will repeat a few more, which you may repeat
after me.   " I was glad when they said unto me,
We will go into the house of the Lord."   Psalm
cxxii. 1 (Prayer-book version).

"Lord, I have loved the habitation of Thy house, and the place where Thine honour dwelleth." Psalm xxvi. 8 (Prayer-book version).

" Even them will I bring to My holy mountain, and make them joyful in My house of prayer; their burnt offerings and their sacrifices shall be accepted upon Mine altar; for Mine house shall be called an house of prayer for all people." Isaiah lvi. 7.

"Where two or three are gathered together in My name, there am I in the midst of them." Matthew xviii. 20.

Who said those last words?—Our Lord Jesus Christ.

Did He go to public worship when He was on earth?—Yes, St. Luke says, "As His custom was He went into the synagogue on the sabbath-day." Luke iv. 16.

Did the Apostles go also?—Yes, they continued "daily with one accord in the Temple." Acts ii. 46.

What is a synagogue?—The house of God where the Jews worshipped.

And what is the Temple?—The Temple was the large, beautiful house of God at Jerusalem where the sacrifices were offered.

And what is our house of God here called?—A church.

And what are very large, beautiful churches called?—Cathedrals, or Minsters.

How should you behave when you go to church?—With very great reverence.

Why?—Because it is God's house, and He is there waiting to receive our worship.

What must you try to do?—Try to join in the Service.

How can you join in it?—By standing, and kneeling, and bowing at the proper places.

And how besides?—By saying aloud all the parts of the Service that the people are meant to say.

How besides?—By trying to mean what I say, and to say it from my heart.

How besides?—By listening attentively to all that the clergyman reads or says.

———◆◆◆———

INTRODUCTION.

Part II.—The Book of Common Prayer.

What does the Prayer-book contain?—All the Services that are used in Church.

Can you tell me any of them?—The Morning and Evening Service.

What besides?—The Litany.

What besides?—The Holy Communion.

Can you think of any other Services in the Prayer-book?—The Services for Baptism, Confirmation, Marriage, Churching of Women, Visitation and Communion of the Sick, and Burial of the Dead.

And what is the name of the Service used on Ash Wednesday?—The Commination Service.

Are there any other Services in the Prayer-book you can think of?—The Ordination Service.

When is the Ordination Service used?—At

Ordination, when, with the laying on of hands and with prayer, men are set apart for the ministry of the Church, and thus receive authority to become pastors of Christ's flock.

How many orders of Clergy are there in the Church?·· Three : Bishops, Priests, and Deacons.

What more does the Prayer-book contain ?—The Collects, Epistles, and Gospels for Sundays and Holy-days.

Anything else ?—The Psalms.

Who wrote the Prayer-book ?—The Prayer-book was not written by one man; the prayers in it are, for the most part, collected and arranged from very old liturgies.

What do you mean by liturgies ? — Forms of public service.

Were there any old liturgies used by the Church soon after the Apostles' time ?—Yes, there were several.

Was the Church founded in our country before St. Augustine was sent here in the year 596 ?—Yes; the British Church was founded some time earlier. We learn * that in the year 314 there were three British bishops, of York, London, and Caerleon, attending with their priests and deacons a General Council of the Church at Arles, in France. So the Church in Britain must as early as 314 have been established, spread in a measure over the land, and in full communion with the rest of the Church of Christ.

Was not the light of the British Church nearly put out when Britain was conquered by the

* Crake's "History of the Church"; Lea on the Prayer-book.

heathen Saxons?—Yes, but it was never entirely extinguished, and at the very time when St. Augustine was sent over by St. Gregory to convert the Saxons in the South, the great St. Columba of Iona was upholding the faith in the North of Britain.

What forms of public worship did St. Augustine bring with him?—The Apostles' Creed, probably the Athanasian Creed, the Te Deum, and a great many of our Prayers and Collects, and with these he arranged a liturgy. At the Norman Conquest this liturgy was revised, and one of the chief liturgies arranged from it, called the Use of Sarum, was generally used until the Reformation.

What do you mean by the Reformation?—I mean the time when, more than three hundred years ago, the Church in this country, freeing itself from the power which the Popes of Rome had gradually (but not till after the 10th century) usurped over other Churches, was cleansed and purified from many false doctrines and wrong practices which had crept into it, and was again made like what it was in the times of the early Christians.

Our English Church was not, then, founded at the time of the Reformation?—Certainly not. Its being reformed and cleansed did not make it a new Church.

Was the Prayer-book made at the time of the Reformation?—No, it was arranged by the bishops and clergy chiefly from the old liturgies or Service-books, and it was all put into English so that everybody might understand it.

In what year was the Prayer-book thus arranged?—In 1549, and again in 1552; and some alterations were made in 1603 and 1662.

All this is rather hard for you to understand. Why have I told it you?—That I may remember that our Creeds and Prayers are not new, but have been used by the Church from very early times.

Is it a good thing to have a Prayer-book, containing forms of prayer to be used in church?—Yes.

For what reasons?—Because we could not all join together in our worship unless we had a form of Service arranged.

If the Minister were to pray in his own words, and the Congregation did not know beforehand what he was going to say, could that be called common prayer?—No, for it would be one man's prayer, not the prayer of the whole congregation.

For what other reason is a form of Service desirable?—That there may be no fear of our using words that are not careful and reverent when we approach God, and that no false doctrine may be brought into our prayers and praises.

Can you give another reason why it is a good thing to have a Prayer-book, with forms of service in it?—Because when we use it we know that we are worshipping in the same manner, and with the same words with thousands of our fellow-Christians at the same time. And not only so, but in the same words that many Christians have used for hundreds of years. Thus we are able to understand in part what is the meaning of the Communion of Saints.

Did our Lord Himself use forms of Service? —Yes, for the Jews had forms of Service, and our Lord must have joined in them when He worshipped in the synagogues.

Can you tell me what part of our Service was used by the Jews?—The Psalms.

Did our Lord give us any forms of prayer?— Yes, the Lord's Prayer; and He not only said, "When ye pray, say, Our Father," but He also said, "After this manner therefore pray ye," teaching us thus that we might use other forms of prayer.

THE MORNING SERVICE.

LESSON I.

Open your Prayer-books at the Morning Service.—Read the Title.—"The Order for Morning Prayer, daily throughout the Year."

What does Order mean?—Rule, or arrangement.

What is the other name used in the Prayer-book for Morning Prayer?—Matins.

Then what does Matins mean?—Morning Prayer, or Morning Service.

Into how many parts may the Morning Service be divided?—Into three parts.

What are they?—1. The Introduction. 2. The Service of Praise. 3. The Service of Prayer.

What is the highest sort of worship?—Praise.

Then why do we not begin with praise?— Because we are not fit to praise God until we have confessed our sins, sought for pardon, and received absolution for them.

What part of the Morning Service forms the Introduction ?—The Sentences, the Exhortation, the General Confession, the Absolution, the Lord's Prayer, and the first set of Versicles and Responses.

Where does the Service of Praise begin ?—When we stand up, and the Priest begins " Glory be to the Father, and to the Son, and to the Holy Ghost."

Is there anything included in this part of the Service besides praise ?—Yes, the hearing of God's Holy Word.

Where does the Service of Praise end, and the Service of Prayer begin ?—After the Apostles' Creed.

All through the Service, at the head of every short portion, you find some lines written in italics, or slanting letters, what are these ?—They are called the Rubrics.

What are the Rubrics ?—The directions for conducting the Service.

Whom are the directions for ?—Both for the Minister and for the People.

What sort of directions are given to them ?—About the position of body in which they are to worship, standing, or kneeling.

And what else ?—About their voices, whether the Minister alone is to speak, or whether the People are to join with him.

Why are these directions called Rubrics ?—From a Latin word meaning red; they used to be written in red letters, and are still in some Prayer-books so written.

LESSON II.—THE SENTENCES.

Read the Rubric.—"At the beginning of Morning Prayer the Minister shall read with a loud voice some one or more of these Sentences of the Scriptures that follow. And then he shall say that which is written after the said Sentences."

What does the Minister do at the beginning of Morning Prayer?—He stands and reads.

What do the People do?—They stand and listen.

Are they to repeat the Sentences with their lips?—No, they are to listen only.

Why do they stand?—To show respectful attention to God's Word.

Why does the Minister stand?—Because he is delivering a message.

How many Sentences are there?—Eleven.

Are they all read?—Only one or two, generally, at once.

Where do all the Sentences come from?—From the Scriptures.

What are they all about?—They are all invitations to us to repent of our sins.

Read the first Sentence.—"When the wicked man turneth away from his wickedness that he hath committed, and doeth that which is lawful and right, he shall save his soul alive."

Where is this verse taken from?—From the prophet Ezekiel.

What does "turning away from wickedness" mean?—Leaving it off, never doing it again.

If a man really repents, what must he do besides

leaving off sin ?—He must do that which is lawful and right.

What is meant by "save his soul alive"?—Procuring life and salvation through our Saviour Jesus Christ.

Read the second Sentence.—"I acknowledge my transgressions, and my sin is ever before me."

Where is this sentence taken from ?—From the 51st Psalm.

What part of repentance is put before us here ?—Confession.

Are we going to acknowledge our transgressions ?—Yes, we do so in the General Confession.

What did David mean when he said, "My sin is ever before me ?"—That he never forgot how he had sinned against God.

Read the third Sentence.—"Hide Thy face from my sins, and blot out all mine iniquities."

Where is this sentence taken from ?—From the 51st Psalm.

What does, "Hide Thy face from my sins" mean ?—Do not look at them.

What are iniquities ?—Evil deeds.

What does "blot them out" mean?—Blot them out of Thy book in which they are written down, so that they can be read there no more.

Read the fourth Sentence.—"The sacrifices of God are a broken spirit : a broken and a contrite heart, O God, Thou wilt not despise."

Where is this sentence taken from?—From the same Psalm as the two Sentences before.

When was it written ?—It was written by David when he was in great sorrow for the sin for which Nathan had reproved him. It is one of the Seven Penitential Psalms.

What is a sacrifice ?—Something we offer to God.

What is a broken spirit ?—A spirit so broken of its pride (that is broken in, or tamed) that it comes humbly to confess its sin.

What is a contrite heart ?—A heart full of repentance, worn down with sorrow for sin.

What do you understand by God not "despising" such a heart and spirit ?—That He will not turn away from them, but will in pity receive them.

Read the fifth Sentence :—" Rend your heart, and not your garments, and turn unto the Lord your God : for He is gracious and merciful, slow to anger, and of great kindness, and repenteth Him of the evil."

Where is this sentence taken from ?—From the prophet Joel.

What is to " rend ".?—To tear.

What are " garments " ?—Clothes.

Did you ever read of anyone rending his garments ?—Yes, it was a common custom when people were in great trouble or sorrow.

Give me an instance.—Reuben rent his clothes when he found that Joseph was no longer in the pit.

What, then, does " rend your hearts " mean ? —Have inward sorrow, instead of outward.

What promise does this text contain ?—That if we are truly sorry and return to God, He will have mercy upon us.

How does the prophet describe His mercy ?—He says that, " He is gracious and merciful,—slow to anger,—of great kindness,—and repenteth Him of the evil."

What does " repenteth Him of the evil" mean ?
—That He will not send the evil upon us which
He had intended to send.

Read the sixth Sentence : — " To the Lord
our God belong mercies and forgivenesses,
though we have rebelled against Him : neither have we obeyed the voice of the Lord
our God, to walk in His laws which He set
before us."

Where is this sentence taken from ?—From
the prophet Daniel.

Whose sins was Daniel confessing ?—The sins
of the Jewish nation.

Of what does this text assure us ?—Of the
mercy and forgiveness of God.

What is rebellion ?—Wilful disobedience.

When did we promise " to walk in His laws
which He set before us " ?—At our Baptism,
when we promised to " keep God's holy will and
commandments, and walk in the same all the
days of our life."

Read the seventh Sentence:—" O Lord, correct
me, but with judgment; not in Thine anger, lest
Thou bring me to nothing."

Where are these words found ?—Both in the
6th Psalm, and in the prophet Jeremiah.

What does " correct me with judgment "
mean ?—Punish me only as far as Thou seest I
can bear.

What could God do with us in His anger if
it pleased Him ?—Destroy us in a moment.

Read the eighth Sentence :—" Repent ye ; for
the Kingdom of Heaven is at hand."

Where does this sentence come from ?—From
the Gospel of St. Matthew.

By whom were the words said?—First by St. John the Baptist, and afterwards by our Lord.

What did they mean by "the Kingdom of Heaven"?—The Kingdom which our Lord was about to set up on earth—viz., His Church.

When was the Church of Christ set up?—On the day of Pentecost.

Read the ninth Sentence:—"I will arise, and go to my father, and will say unto him, Father, I have sinned against Heaven, and before thee, and am no more worthy to be called thy son."

Where is this sentence taken from?—From the Parable of the Prodigal Son in the Gospel of St. Luke.

What does it teach us?—That when we have once by baptism been placed in our Father's house (in that Kingdom of Heaven set up by our Lord) and then leave it like the Prodigal Son, the only way of return to it is the way of repentance.

Read the tenth Sentence:—"Enter not into judgment with Thy servant, O Lord; for in Thy sight shall no man living be justified."

Where do we find this sentence?—In the 143rd Psalm.

What is it we pray God not to do?—Not to "enter into judgment" with us.

What is the object of this prayer?—That He may not judge us, and try our actions whether they be good or evil.

Why not?—Because we could not bear it, for in His holy sight the best man living could not be accounted just.

Read the eleventh Sentence:—"If we say that

we have no sin, we deceive ourselves, and the truth is not in us ; but, if we confess our sins, He is faithful and just to forgive us our sins, and to cleanse us from all unrighteousness."

Where is this last sentence taken from ?—From the 1st Epistle of St. John.

What does it declare ?—That we cannot be speaking the truth if we say we have no sin.

And what else ?—That if we confess our sins God will forgive us, and wash away the guilt of them.

Why does the text say that " He is faithful and just to forgive us our sins " ?—Faithful and just in keeping His promises, that He will forgive our sins if we repent.

What is the first means of being cleansed from sin ?—Holy Baptism.

Can we be baptized a second time to wash away our after-sins ?—No, there is only " one baptism for the remission of sins."

How then can our sins after baptism be cleansed ?—Just as our Lord said, " He that is washed needeth not save to wash his feet " ; so it is by repentant tears, and faith in the Blood of Christ, that baptized Christians whose feet are daily soiled by walking amongst the defilements of this world, must daily repent and be cleansed.

What does our Saviour do for us in order that we may obtain this pardon ?—He intercedes for us. "If any man sin " (that is, after Baptism), " we have an advocate with the Father, Jesus Christ, the righteous."

LESSON III.—THE EXHORTATION.

What follows the Sentences?—The Exhortation.

What is an Exhortation?—An urgent address.
Who reads the Exhortation?—The Minister.
To whom does he read it?—To the People.
What do they do?—They stand and listen.
Ought they to repeat the words after the Minister?—No, they should only attentively listen.

What is the Exhortation about?—It is a short sermon on the texts just read. First, we are exhorted to confess our sins,—then we are told we ought especially to do so in church,—and then the different parts of worship for which we come to church are mentioned. And at the end of the Exhortation the Minister prays us to begin our worship by joining him in confessing our sins.

Read the first part of the Exhortation:—
" Dearly beloved brethren, the Scripture moveth us in sundry places to acknowledge and confess our manifold sins and wickedness; and that we should not dissemble nor cloke them before the face of Almighty God our heavenly Father; but confess them with an humble, lowly, penitent, and obedient heart; to the end that we may obtain forgiveness of the same, by His infinite goodness and mercy."

How does the Minister address the Congregation? — He calls them " Dearly beloved brethren."

Whose example is here followed?—The example of St. Paul, who thus addresses the Christians at Philippi.   Phil. iv. 1.

How are they his brethren?—Because all are children of one Father.

What does he tell them?—That the Scripture moves us in sundry places to acknowledge and confess our manifold sins and wickedness.

What is it to "move" a person?—To call upon him and stir him up to do anything.

What is meant by "sundry places"?—Different places.

Can you think of any places in Scripture where we are moved to confess our sins?—All the sentences of Scripture which come before the Exhortation move us to do so.

What is to "acknowledge" a sin?—To own that we have done it.

And what is to "confess" a sin?—To tell it before God.

How are our sins described here?—As "manifold sins and wickedness."

What are "manifold sins"?—Many sins done over and over again.

What does the Minister exhort us not to do?—Not to dissemble nor cloke them before the face of Almighty God our Heavenly Father.

What does "dissemble" mean?—To pretend to be different from what we are.

What is to "cloke" our sins?—To try to hide them; as if a man were to cover ragged clothes with a cloak.   John xv. 22.

Why is God here spoken of under the title of

" Almighty " God ?—To remind us that He is able to punish us for our sins.

And why is He at the same time called " our Heavenly Father ? "—To remind us of His love and His willingness to pardon.

Instead of dissembling and cloking our sins, what are we bidden to do ?—To confess them, with an humble, lowly, penitent, and obedient heart.

What is an " humble " heart ?—A heart that feels its unworthiness.

What is a " lowly " heart ?—A heart that thinks others better than itself.

What is a " penitent " heart ?—A heart that repents of its sins.

What is an " obedient " heart ?—A heart that resolves to obey God for the future.

And for what purpose does the Minister exhort us to confess our sins ?—To the end that we may obtain forgiveness of the same by His infinite goodness and mercy.

What is meant by the " same "?—The (same) manifold sins and wickedness we are going to confess.

What are the goodness and mercy of God here called ?—Infinite.

What does that mean ?—Unbounded, without end. Psalm cxxxvi. 1.

Read the next part of the Exhortation.— " And although we ought at all times humbly to acknowledge our sins before God ; yet ought we most chiefly so to do when we assemble and meet together to render thanks for the great benefits that we have received at His hands, to set forth

His most worthy praise, to hear His most holy Word, and to ask those things which are requisite and necessary, as well for the body as the soul."

When ought we to "acknowledge our sins" towards God?—At all times.

But when is the especial time for doing so?—When we assemble and meet together.

For what purpose?—To worship God.

Where do we assemble to worship God?—At church.

What are the four parts of worship mentioned in the Exhortation?—First, to render thanks for the great benefits that we have received at God's hands.

What is "rendering thanks"?—Returning thanks.

What are "benefits"?—Good things.

Whereabouts in the Morning Service do we render thanks?—In the General Thanksgiving.

What is the second part of worship mentioned?—To set forth God's most worthy praise.

What does "worthy" mean?—Well-deserved.

In what parts of the Service do we praise God?—In the Psalms and the Canticles.

What is the third part?—To hear His most holy Word.

In what parts of the Service do we hear His most holy Word?—In the Psalms and Lessons, and afterwards in the Commandments and the Epistle and Gospel.

And what is the last part of worship mentioned in the Exhortation?—To ask those things which are requisite and necessary, as well for the body as the soul.

In what part of the Service do we do this?—In the prayers.

What does "requisite" mean?—Wanted.

Why does prayer for our own needs form the last part of worship?—Because our Saviour taught us in the Lord's Prayer to think of God's honour before our own wants.

Read the rest of the Exhortation.—"Wherefore I pray and beseech you, as many as are here present, to accompany me with a pure heart, and humble voice, unto the throne of the heavenly grace, saying after me."

What does "wherefore" mean?—For this reason.

For what reason?—Because the Scripture bids us confess our many sins to God.

And for this reason what does the Minister pray and beseech us all to do?—To accompany him to the throne of the heavenly grace.

What does this mean?—To join with him in prayer to God our King.

What does "beseech" mean?—To beg earnestly.

What is the throne of God sometimes called?—The throne of grace, or the mercy-seat.

Why is it so called?—To assure us that we may come boldly to it, and obtain mercy through the blood of Christ our High Priest. Heb. iv. 14–16.

In what manner does the Minister bid us accompany him?—With a pure heart.

Does this mean a heart clean from sin?—No; for we are coming burdened with sin.

What does it mean, then ?—A heart pure in intention, that hates sin and intends to leave it off.

What else are we to come with ?—With a humble voice.

What is that ?—A quiet and lowly voice.

What does the Minister mean by the words, " saying after me " ?—That the People are to repeat after him each sentence of the Confession that follows.

———◆◇◆———

LESSON IV.—THE GENERAL CONFESSION.

What follows the Exhortation ?—The General Confession.

Why is this Confession called " General " ?—Because it is not a confession of any particular sins, but of general sins, which the whole Congregation can join in confessing.

Read the rubric.—" To be said of the whole Congregation after the Minister, all kneeling."

Who repeats the General Confession ?—The Minister repeats it first, and the Congregation repeat it aloud after him.

In what posture of body are they all to be ?—All kneeling.

Why should they kneel ?—Because it is the natural position of sinners asking mercy from God.

Can you think of a verse in the Bible which bids us kneel ?—" O come, let us worship, and fall down ; and kneel before the Lord our Maker." Psalm xcv. 6 (Prayer-book version).

If you have no stool to kneel upon, will that

excuse you from kneeling?—No; I can kneel on the floor. Our Lord knelt on the ground in the garden, and St. Paul knelt on the sea-shore. Mark xiv. 35; Luke xxii. 41; Acts xx. 36.

How do we address God in the General Confession?—Almighty and most merciful Father.

Why do we in this place call God our "Father" in the full meaning of the word?—Because, like as a father pities and forgives his children, so we trust that our Heavenly Father will have pity on us. Psalm ciii. 8, 13 (Prayer-book version).

When did we first gain the right to call Him "Father"?—At our baptism, when we were made His children.

And why do we call Him "Almighty" and "Most Merciful"?—"Almighty" because He is able to forgive our sins, and "Most Merciful" because He is willing.

Read the Confession.—"We have erred and strayed from thy ways like lost sheep. We have followed too much the devices and desires of our own hearts. We have offended against Thy holy laws. We have left undone those things which we ought to have done; and we have done those things which we ought not to have done; and there is no health in us."

What is "erred"?—Wandered.

Where are we compared in the Bible to wandering sheep?—In the fifty-third chapter of Isaiah: "All we like sheep have gone astray."

And where besides?—In the parable of the Lost Sheep.

What have we " erred and strayed" from ?—
From God's ways.

What are His ways ?—The ways of His commandments, the narrow path we have promised to walk in.

What have we followed too much instead ?—The devices and desires of our own hearts.

What are the " devices " of our own hearts ?—Our own plans.

What are the " desires " of our own hearts ?—Our own wishes.

And what has following our own plans and wishes caused us to do ?—To offend against God's holy laws.

What does that mean ?—To stumble against and break God's holy laws.

In what two ways have we broken God's holy laws ?—We have left undone those things which we ought to have done; and we have done those things which we ought not to have done.

What are these sins called ?—Sins of omission, and sins of commission.

What does omission mean ?— Omitting, or leaving undone.

What does commission mean ?—Committing, or doing.

Which is the worst sin, to leave undone what we ought to do, or to do what we ought not to do ?—Men think very little of leaving undone what they ought to do, but in the sight of God it is probably as wicked as doing what we ought not to do.

Where are we taught so ?—In the account of the Last Judgment (Matt. xxv.) those who were placed on the left hand were placed there because they had left undone what they ought to have done.

In what parable are we taught the same ?—In the parable of the Talents.

How do we finish our confession ?—By saying " And there is no health in us."

What sort of health is meant ?—Spiritual health, health of the soul.

After we have confessed these sins, what do we next do ?—We beg God to spare and forgive us.

Read the words.—" But Thou, O Lord, have mercy upon us, miserable offenders. Spare Thou them, O God, which confess their faults. Restore Thou them that are penitent ; according to Thy promises declared unto mankind in Christ Jesu our Lord."

What do we beg for ?—For mercy, although we have sinned so much : " But Thou, O Lord, have mercy upon us." Psalm li. 1.

What do we call ourselves ?—Miserable offenders.

What does "miserable" mean ?—To be pitied.

What do we next ask Him to do ?—Spare Thou them, O God, which confess their faults.

Have we done so ?—Yes, we have just been confessing our faults.

What does "spare" mean ?—Deliver from punishment.

What is our next prayer ?—Restore Thou them that are penitent.

What does "restore" mean ?—Place back again.

Who are the "penitent"?—Those who are really sorry.

What do we mean, then, when we ask God to restore them that are penitent?—To place them again in the right path, from which they have erred, and restore them to His favour.

How can we hope that God will have mercy upon us, spare us, and restore us?—Because He has promised it.

So how do we ask Him to do it?—According to Thy promises declared unto mankind in Christ Jesu our Lord.

How were these promises of mercy through Christ declared unto mankind?—They were promised beforehand by sacrifices, and types, and prophecies. And then they were declared by Christ Himself and His apostles.

How is the General Confession finished?—By a petition for the future.

Read it. — "And grant, O most merciful Father, for His sake, that we may hereafter live a godly, righteous, and sober life, to the glory of Thy holy name. Amen."

In asking our "merciful Father" to grant us something, why do we say "for His sake," that is, "for Christ's sake"?—Because our Saviour Himself told us that the Father will give us anything we ask, if we ask it in His name. John xvi. 23, 24.

What is it that we ask God to grant?—That we may hereafter live a godly, righteous, and sober life.

What does "hereafter" mean?—From this time forward.

What is a "godly" life ?—A life that is spent in the service of God.

What is a "righteous" life ?—The life of one who does his duty towards his neighbour.

What is a "sober" life ?—The life of one who does his duty towards himself.　Titus ii. 12.

Why do we add, "To the glory of Thy Holy Name"?—Because the glory of God should be the end and reason of all our actions.　1 Cor. x. 31.

And for what other reason ?—Because when a Christian leads a good life he glorifies not himself, but God who gives him the grace to do it. John xv. 8.

What does "Amen" at the end of a prayer mean ?—May it be so.

Lesson V.—The Absolution.

What follows the General Confession ?—The Absolution.

What is it called ?—The Absolution, or Remission of sins.

What does Absolution mean ?—Loosing or setting free.

What does Remission mean ?—Putting away.

What is it that we want to be loosed from, and to be put away from us ?—Our sins.

Read the rubric.—"To be pronounced by the Priest alone, standing, the People still kneeling."

What does "pronounced" mean?—Spoken with authority, as by one who has a right to speak.

Who is to pronounce the Absolution?—The priest.

Why does the rubric say "the Priest" and not "the Minister"?—Because no Minister who is not a Priest may pronounce the Absolution.

Are there any Ministers who are not Priests? Yes, Deacons.

Why may not a Deacon pronounce the Absolution?—Because he has never received authority to do so.

When did the Priest receive authority to do so?—At his Ordination.

Who gave him the authority?—The Bishop.

Can you repeat the Bishop's words from the Ordination Service?—" Receive the Holy Ghost for the Office and Work of a Priest in the Church of God, now committed unto thee by the Imposition of our hands. Whose sins thou dost forgive, they are forgiven; and whose sins thou dost retain, they are retained."

From whom did the Bishop receive this authority?—From the Apostles; they gave it to the Bishops whom they ordained, and it was handed down from Bishop to Bishop to this day.

Who gave the Apostles the authority to absolve sins?—Our Lord Himself. John xx. 22, 23.

Why does the rubric say the Absolution is "to be pronounced by the Priest alone"?—Because the people are not to repeat it after him, they are only to listen.

In what posture are they to be?—The Priest

stands, because he is delivering a message. The People kneel, as humbly listening to it.

Read the first part:—" Almighty God, the Father of our Lord Jesus Christ, who desireth not the death of a sinner, but rather that he may turn from his wickedness, and live ; and hath given power, and commandment, to His Ministers, to declare and pronounce to His people, being penitent, the Absolution and Remission of their sins : He pardoneth and absolveth all them that truly repent, and unfeignedly believe His holy Gospel."

As this is not a prayer, why does it begin thus, " Almighty God " ?—The Priest is not praying *to* God, he is speaking to the People *of* God.

Why should the Priest mention here that He is " the Father of our Lord Jesus Christ " ?— Because he is going to give us the message of pardon, and it is only through our Lord Jesus Christ that God will pardon us.

What is the first thing that the Priest declares about Almighty God ?—That He desireth not the death of a sinner, but rather that he should turn from his wickedness and live.

Where are we told this ?—In the 18th chapter of Ezekiel.

What does " the death of a sinner " mean ?— The death of his soul here, and eternal death hereafter.

What is the next thing that the Priest declares about Almighty God ?—That He " hath given power, and commandment, to His Ministers."

What power and commandment ?—" To declare

and pronounce to His people, being penitent, the Absolution and Remission of their sins."

When did Christ promise to give this power to His Ministers?—When He first spoke to His Apostles of the Church He was going to build, and said to Peter, "I will give unto thee the keys of the Kingdom of Heaven, and whatsoever thou shalt bind on earth shall be bound in Heaven, and whatsoever thou shalt loose on earth shall be loosed in Heaven." Matt. xvi. 19.

Did He promise to give this power to the other Apostles as well as to St. Peter?—Yes, He soon after promised it to them all in the very same words. Matt. xviii. 18.

And when did He give them the power?—After His resurrection, when He breathed on them, and said unto them, "Receive ye the Holy Ghost: whosesoever sins ye remit they are remitted unto them, and whosesoever sins ye retain they are retained." John xx. 22, 23.

To whom are Christ's Ministers to declare and pronounce this Absolution?—To His people.

Who are God's people?—All Christians.

On what condition?—On condition of their "being penitent."

Having declared this, what does the Priest do next?—He pronounces the Absolution in these words, "He pardoneth and absolveth all them that truly repent, and unfeignedly believe His holy Gospel."

Who absolves?—God alone.

What does the priest do?—He declares God's pardon.

What does "absolveth" mean ?—Looses, or sets free.

If we hope to be pardoned and absolved, what two things must we do ?—Truly repent, and unfeignedly believe His holy Gospel.

What is to repent truly ?—Really to intend to leave our sins off; not to pretend to be sorry, and then sin again.

What does "unfeignedly" mean ?—Sincerely.

What is "His holy Gospel"?—The glad tidings brought from Heaven to man of reconciliation to God through Jesus Christ.

What two things then are required of us before we can be pardoned and absolved ?—True repentance and sincere faith.

After the Priest has pronounced this Absolution to those who repent and believe, what does he go on to say ?—"Wherefore let us beseech Him to grant us true repentance, and His Holy Spirit, that those things may please Him, which we do at this present; and that the rest of our life hereafter may be pure, and holy; so that at the last we may come to His eternal joy; through Jesus Christ our Lord."

"Wherefore let us beseech Him"; what does "wherefore" mean ?—For this reason.

For what reason ?—That God absolves those who truly repent and believe.

Why does the Priest say, "let *us* beseech him"? —Because, having delivered his message, he now joins himself with the People.

What should we beseech God to grant us ?—True repentance and His Holy Spirit.

What do we need the Holy Spirit for ?—To

D

make the things which we are doing at this present pleasing to God.

What does " at this present " mean ?—Now, at this present time.

What are we doing now ?—Offering worship to God.

And for what else do we need His Holy Spirit ?—That the rest of our life hereafter may be pure and holy.

What does " hereafter " mean ?—For the future.

If we truly repent and believe, and try to lead such a pure and holy life, what may we hope for ?—That at the last we may come to His eternal joy.

What is that ?—The eternal happiness of Heaven.

How is it that sinners can ever obtain that eternal joy ?—Only " through Jesus Christ our Lord."

Read the rubric at the end of the Absolution. —" The people shall answer here, and at the end of all other prayers, *Amen*."

Why is the Absolution here called a prayer ? —Because the latter part of it is an invitation to prayer, though not itself a prayer.

LESSON VI.—THE LORD'S PRAYER AND VERSICLES.

What follows the Absolution?—The Lord's Prayer.

Why do we use the Lord's Prayer now?—Because, having been purified from our sin by Confession and Absolution, we may now come near to God our Father in our Lord's own words.

Read the rubric.—"Here the Minister shall kneel, and say the Lord's prayer with an audible voice; the People also kneeling, and repeating it with him, both here, and wheresoever else it is used in Divine Service."

What is the Minister directed to do?—To kneel.

Why?—Because he is no longer delivering a message, he is going to pray with the People.

Why is he called a Minister, and not a Priest? —Because any Minister, whether Priest or only Deacon, may lead the prayers of the People.

How is he to say the Lord's Prayer?—With an audible voice.

What is that?—A voice that can be heard.

What are the People to do?—They are to remain kneeling, and repeat the prayer with him.

Why does the rubric say "repeat it *with* him," while in the Confession is said, "repeat it *after* him"?—Because every one, whether he can read or not, knows the Lord's Prayer by heart, and therefore can repeat it *with* him.

Read the Lord's Prayer.

[The Lord's Prayer having been taught and explained in the Church Catechism, it is not considered necessary to give any explanation of it here.]

" Our Father, which art in Heaven, Hallowed be thy Name. Thy kingdom come. Thy will be done in earth, As it is in heaven. Give us this day our daily bread. And forgive us our trespasses, As we forgive them that trespass against us. And lead us not into temptation ; But deliver us from evil ; For Thine is the Kingdom, the Power, and the Glory, for ever and ever.   Amen."

How often is the Lord's Prayer repeated in the Morning Service ?—Twice.

Is it found in any other Service ?—Yes, in every Service in the Prayer-book.

Why is it repeated twice in the Morning Service ?—Because there are two divisions of the Morning Service, a Service of Praise and a Service of Prayer.

Is there any difference in the manner in which we repeat the Lord's Prayer in these two divisions ?—Yes.   We repeat it the first time just as we are going to begin to praise God, and therefore we add the Doxology.   We leave out the Doxology the second time, because we are beginning then the Service of Prayer.

What does " Doxology " mean ?—Words of praise.

What are the words of the Doxology ?—" For Thine is the kingdom, the power, and the glory, for ever and ever."

Do we add the Doxology to the Lord's Prayer in any other Service in the Prayer-book ?—

Yes; but only in those which are Services of Praise.

Which are they?—The first part of the Evening Service, the second part of the Holy Communion Service, the Churching of Women, and in a Storm at Sea.

What follows the Lord's Prayer?—Two short versicles, with their responses.

What is a versicle?—A little verse.

What is a response?—An answer.

What are we just going to begin?—The Service of Praise.

What is the link between the two?—The Lord's Prayer and the Versicles and Responses.

Read the rubric before the versicles.—"Then likewise he shall say."

Who is "he"?—The Minister.

Read the first versicle.—"O Lord, open Thou our lips."

What is the response of the People?—"And our mouth shall show forth Thy praise."

Where do these words come from?—From Psalm li. 15.

What do they express?—Our want of power to declare God's praise, and our need of His touch to open our dumb mouths.

Read the second versicle.—"O God, make speed to save us."

What is the response of the People?—"O Lord, make haste to help us."

Where do these words come from?—From Psalm lxx. 1.

LESSON VII.—THE GLORIA PATRI.

What part of the Service is now finished ?—The Introduction.

And what begins now ?—The Service of Praise.

Read the rubric.—" Here all standing up, the Priest shall say."

Why do the Priest and People all stand ?—Because they are going to praise God, and standing is the proper posture of praise.

Are there any directions in the rubric for changing this standing posture during the Service of Praise ?—None, until the end of the Apostles' Creed, when the Service of Praise is over.

Why then do we sit down during the Lessons ?—It has become the custom to do so, but there is no direction for it. We still, however, stand to hear the Word of God during the Gospel in the Communion Service.

How is the Service of Praise begun ?—With the Gloria Patri.

Read the words of the Gloria Patri.—" Glory be to the Father, and to the Son, and to the Holy Ghost; As it was in the beginning, is now, and ever shall be, world without end. Amen."

Why is this called the Gloria Patri ?—They are the two first words of it in Latin, and mean " Glory to the Father."

What is it also called ?—The Doxology.

To whom do we give glory in the " Gloria Patri " ?—To the Holy Trinity.

Where in the Bible are we first taught to give glory to the Trinity ?—In the song of the angels recorded by Isaiah, " One cried unto another and said, Holy, Holy, Holy, is the Lord of Hosts." Isaiah vi. 3.

Where in the New Testament do we hear of three Persons in one Godhead ?—Just before our Lord's Ascension, when He bids His apostles make disciples of all nations, " baptizing them in the name of the Father, and of the Son, and of the Holy Ghost."

By whom was Glory sung " in the beginning"? —By the angels " when the morning stars sang together, and all the sons of God shouted for joy." Job xxxviii. 7.

By whom is it sung " now "?—By the angels in heaven, by the Church in Paradise, and by the Church militant on earth.

And by whom " shall it ever be " sung ?—By the Church triumphant in heaven.

What does " world without end " mean ?— Through all eternity.

After the Gloria Patri what does the Priest call upon the People to do ?—" Praise ye the Lord."

And in what words do they agree ?—" The Lord's Name be praised."

Why do this versicle and answer follow the Gloria Patri ?—Because, as we have just acknowledged the Trinity of the Godhead, we now acknowledge the Unity, that the Father, and the Son, and the Holy Ghost are one Lord.

LESSON VIII.—THE VENITE.

What Song of Praise follows the Gloria Patri ? —The 95th Psalm.

What is it generally called ?—The Venite.

What words stand at the head of it ?—Venite, exultemus Domino.

What do these words mean ?—They are the first words of the Psalm in Latin.

What is this Psalm also called ?—The Invitatory, or Invitation Psalm.

Why is it so called ?—Because it invites us to worship God.

Read the rubric.—"Then shall be said or sung this Psalm following ; except on Easter-Day, upon which another Anthem is appointed : and on the Nineteenth Day of every Month it is not to be read here, but in the ordinary course of the Psalms."

On what days only is the Venite not to be used ? — On Easter-Day and the day of the Queen's Accession.

Why not on these days ? — Because special Anthems are appointed for these days, which are used instead.

Where do we find these Anthems ?—At the head of the Collect for Easter-Day, and in the Prayers for the Queen's Accession (*June* 20).

Why is the Venite not used here on the 19th day of the month ?—Because it comes in the Psalms for the day, and is not to be used twice over.

How is the Venite to be repeated?—It is to be "said or sung."

If it is said, who says it?—The Minister and People, each saying a verse in turn.

And how may it be sung?—It may be either simply chanted, and each side of the choir may take a verse in turn, or it may be sung in a less simple way.

Read the first verse.—"O come, let us sing unto the Lord : let us heartily rejoice in the strength of our salvation."

How do we begin the Psalm?—We invite and call upon each other to sing praises and rejoice in the Lord.

What name do we give to the Lord in this verse?—The strength of our salvation.

What does that mean?—That He is mighty to save us.

Read the second verse.—"Let us come before His presence with thanksgiving : and show ourselves glad in Him with Psalms."

When do we come before His presence?—When we meet in church.

Why there?—Because it is His house; and He has promised to meet us there.

And what should we bring with us?—Our grateful thanksgiving.

And how can we express our thanksgiving and gladness?—By singing Psalms.

Read the third verse.—"For the Lord is a great God : and a great King above all gods."

What reason is given in this verse for honouring God with praise and thanksgiving?—Because of His greatness and majesty, and that He is the one true God.

Read the fourth verse.—" In His hand are all the corners of the earth : and the strength of the hills is His also."

What are the " corners of the earth " ?—The farthest bounds of the earth.

What is meant by the " strength of the hills"? —The strong foundations of the hills.

In what manner are these " in His hand " ? —As He made them at first, so He still sustains and upholds them.

Read the fifth verse.—" The sea is His, and He made it, and His hands prepared the dry land."

For what do we praise God in this verse ?—For the Creation.

When did He " prepare the dry land " ?— When He said, " Let the waters under the heaven be gathered together unto one place, and let the dry land appear."

Read the sixth verse.—"O come, let us worship, and fall down, and kneel before the Lord our Maker."

What still greater reason does this verse give us for worshipping God ?—That He is the Creator of mankind, our Maker.

How should His creatures approach their Maker ?—With great reverence, falling down and kneeling before Him.

Read the seventh verse.—" For He is the Lord our God : and we are the people of His pasture, and the sheep of His hand."

What is He to His people ?—The Lord their God.

And what are we to Him ?—His people and His sheep.

What is a pasture ?—A feeding-place for sheep.

In the Confession we acknowledged ourselves to be lost sheep, but when He has restored and brought us back, what does our Shepherd do for us ?—Feeds us in His pasture, and keeps us in His hand.

What do the remaining four verses of this Psalm warn us against ?—Against following the bad example of God's first chosen flock.

Who were they ?—The Israelites.

Read the eighth verse.—"To-day if ye will hear His voice, harden not your hearts : as in the provocation, and as in the day of temptation in the wilderness."

What is the surest way of making our hearts hard ?—Hearing God's voice, and not doing as His voice bids us.

How soon ought we to obey ?—To-day, that is, directly we hear ; for the more we put off obeying His voice, the more our hearts get hardened against it.

When did the Israelites harden their hearts ? —When they were in the wilderness.

What was " the provocation " ?—The time when they provoked God.

What was "the day of temptation " ?—The time when they tempted God, that is, tried His patience.

Read the ninth verse.—" When your fathers tempted Me, proved Me, and saw My works."

Who are meant by " your fathers " ?—The Israelites, who were fathers to those in whose time this Psalm was written; and, as God's first people, were in one sense our fathers too.

What did they do?—Tempted and proved God.

How could they do that?—By trying to see how long His mercy and long-suffering would last.

What "works" did they see?—The wonders which God worked in the midst of them.

Read the tenth verse.—"Forty years long was I grieved with this generation, and said : It is a people that do err in their hearts, for they have not known My ways."

How long did they grieve God in the Wilderness?—Forty years.

What does "this generation" mean?—The set of Israelites then living.

What did God say of them?—That they erred in their hearts.

What does "erred" mean?—Went wrong.

In which of our Services is it declared that the curse of God rests on those who "in their hearts go from the Lord"?—In the Commination Service.

What did they refuse to know?—God's ways.

Read the last verse. — "Unto whom I sware in My wrath : that they should not enter into My rest."

What does "wrath" mean?—Anger.

What did God swear in His anger?—That these Israelites should not enter into His rest.

What was "His rest"?—The land of Canaan.

Where are we told that these words of the

95th Psalm should be a warning to Christians?
—In the third and fourth chapters of the Epistle
to the Hebrews.

What is the rest prepared for Christians?—
The rest laid up for us in heaven.

Through what wilderness are we now travel-
ling?—The wilderness of this world.

What must we beware of?—Of provoking God
by hardening our hearts against His voice.

If we do harden our hearts what are we tempt-
ing God to do?—To take away from us our
heavenly inheritance.

How is the Venite ended?—With the Gloria
Patri.

LESSON IX.—THE PSALMS.

After the Venite, in what words do we still go
on praising God?—In the words of the Psalms.

During the singing or reading of the Psalms,
in what posture of body do the Minister and
People remain?—Still standing, because they are
still praising.

Read the rubric.—"Then shall follow the
Psalms in order as they are appointed. And at
the end of every Psalm throughout the year,
and likewise at the end of Benedicite, Benedictus, Magnificat, and Nunc Dimittis, shall be
repeated, Glory be to the Father, and to the
Son, and to the Holy Ghost; As it was in the
beginning, is now, and ever shall be : world without end. Amen."

Where do you find the Psalms ?—Nearly at the end of the Prayer-book.

What is the Book of Psalms sometimes called ? —The Psalter.

In what order are they appointed to be read ? They are to be read through once every month.

How many Psalms are there ?—One hundred and fifty.

And into how many portions are these divided ? —Into thirty mornings and thirty evenings.

And if there are thirty-one days in the month, what are read on the thirty-first day ?—The same portions that were appointed for the day before.

Which Psalm is it that is so long that it is itself divided into portions, and only a few of these read at a time ?—The One Hundred and Nineteenth.

How do we know that the Psalms are appointed to be read in this order ?—Because we find a rubric in the beginning of the Prayer-book, called "The order how the Psalter is appointed to be read," and we are told so there.

What is to be repeated at the end of each Psalm, and each portion of the 119th Psalm ?— The Gloria Patri.

Where does the rubric say the Gloria Patri is to be used besides ? —At the end of all the canticles excepting the Te Deum.

Why is it not repeated at the end of the Te Deum ? — Because the Te Deum contains in itself a doxology to the Holy Trinity.

Where do the Psalms come from ?—From the Old Testament.

Are the Psalms in the Prayer-book in exactly the same words as the Psalms in the Bible ?—No.

How is that ?—Because the Old Testament has been translated from Hebrew into English several times, and the Prayer-book Psalms are an earlier translation than the Bible Psalms.

Why is every verse of the Psalms divided into two parts by a colon ?—In order that it may be chanted, for all chants are divided into two parts.

What are the Psalms called in the Prayer-book ?—The Psalms of David.

Were they all written by King David ?—No ; but he wrote a great many of them ; and for this reason he is called " the sweet Psalmist of Israel." 2 Sam. xxiii. 1.

Into how many books may they be divided ? —Into five books, each of which, with some exceptions, may be considered as belonging to five different periods.

When is the first book said to have been compiled ?—Some have thought in the time of David ; it ends with the 41st Psalm, and all the Psalms in it, except four, bear his name.

When is the second book said to have been compiled ?—In the time of King Hezekiah ; it ends with the 72nd Psalm, and most of the Psalms in it, it would seem, were written by David, and one by Solomon.

And the third ?—In the reign of King Josiah, ending with the 89th Psalm. Of this book one Psalm, the 86th, bears the name of David.

And the fourth ?—During the Captivity ; it ends with the 106th Psalm.

And when, in the opinion of some, was the last book compiled ?—After the return from the Captivity.

Is there anything that marks the close of each of these five books ?—Yes, they all end with a doxology ; that is, with words of praise to the Lord.

Which Psalm was written by Solomon ?—The 72nd, beginning " Give the king thy judgments, O Lord."

Which is said to have been written by Moses ? — The 90th, beginning " Lord, thou hast been our refuge from one generation to another."

Which are the Passover Psalms ? — The six Psalms from the 113th to the 118th. They form the great Hallel or Office of Praise at the Passover. The 113th, 114th, and 115th were sung before the Supper, and the 116th, 117th, and 118th after it. Our Lord and His Apostles thus sung them. Matt. xxvi. 30.

Which are Processional Psalms ?—The 120th to the 134th; they are called Psalms of Degrees (which means " steps "), and were sung by the bands of pilgrims going up to Jerusalem at the feasts, or when ascending the stairs of the Temple.

Which are the Hallelujah Psalms ?—The five last, from the 146th to the 150th ; they are so called because they all begin with the words " Praise the Lord."

Are the Psalms about any different subjects ? —Yes.

Can they be classed according to these subjects?—Yes, we may class six different sorts of Psalms under six different heads.

What are these six subjects?—Psalms of Praise, of Thanksgiving, and of Prayer; Historical Psalms, Instructive Psalms, and Prophetical Psalms.

Can you tell me a few of the Psalms of Praise?—The 8th, 19th, 93rd, 103rd, 104th, 119th, and many more.

What is the particular subject of praise in the 119th Psalm?—The excellence of God's law.

Tell me a few of the Psalms of Thanksgiving.—The 9th, 18th, 30th, 34th, &c., are Psalms of Thanksgiving for separate persons, and the 46th, 48th, 65th, 66th, and many more, of Thanksgiving for the Church.

Are there many Psalms of Prayer?—Yes, very many. Some in affliction, as the 4th and 5th; some entreating help, as the 7th and 17th; some intercessory, as the 20th and the 122nd; some in penitence, as the Seven Penitential Psalms.

What are the Penitential Psalms?—The 6th, 32nd, 38th, 51st, 102nd, 130th, and 143rd.

Which are the Historical Psalms?—There are three; the 78th, the 105th, and the 106th.

What are the Instructive Psalms?—Some speak of the vanity of human life, as the 39th and 90th; some give advice to men in power, as the 82nd and 101st; some speak of the characters and end of good and bad men, as the 1st, 37th, and 58th.

Which are the chief Prophetical Psalms?—Those that point plainly to the Messiah.

Can you mention any of them?—The 2nd

E

Psalm is the plainest of all the Prophetical Psalms. It speaks of the Lord's Anointed, the only-begotten Son of God, being taken before earthly kings and rulers, and of the vanity of all their attempts to stop the spread of His Kingdom, which shall extend to the ends of the earth, for all must submit to Him who is the King of Kings.

Which Psalm prophesies our Lord's Crucifixion ?—The 22nd.

Which His Resurrection ?—The 16th and the 118th.

Which His Ascension ?—The 24th and the 68th.

Which His Session ?—The 110th.

How can we be quite certain that the words in these Psalms were really intended as prophecies of the Messiah ?—Because they are quoted as such by the Evangelists and Apostles in the New Testament.

Are there any days in the year when Psalms on particular subjects are chosen for the Church Service instead of the Psalms for the day ?—Yes, on Christmas-Day, Ash-Wednesday, Good Friday, Easter-Day, Ascension-Day, and Whit-Sunday.

What sorts of Psalms are chosen for those days ?— For Ash-Wednesday, six Penitential Psalms (the seventh being read in the Commination Service) ; and for the other days, Psalms prophetical of the Coming, the Death, the Resurrection, and the Ascension of the Messiah, and of the blessings He has shed upon His people.

LESSON X.—THE FIRST LESSON.

What part of the Morning Service are we now considering ?—The Service of Praise.

What is included in the Service of Praise ? Hearing God's Word.

What is it then that follows the Psalms ?—The First Lesson.

Read the rubric.—"Then shall be read distinctly with an audible voice the First Lesson, taken out of the Old Testament, as is appointed in the Calendar, except there be proper Lessons assigned for that day: He that readeth so standing and turning himself, as he may best be heard of all such as are present. And after that, shall be said or sung, in English, the Hymn called Te Deum Laudamus, daily throughout the year."

Does the rubric say that the Minister is to read the First Lesson ?—No ; therefore any one whom he may appoint may read it for him.

In what way is the reader to read it ?—Distinctly, with an audible voice.

What is " distinctly " ?—Clearly.

And what does " an audible voice " mean ?—A voice that can be heard.

What is the meaning of the word " Lesson " ? A reading.

Where is the First Lesson always taken from? —From the Old Testament.

What does the word Testament mean ?—Covenant, or agreement.

Why is the first part of the Bible called the Old Testament ?—Because it contains the Old Covenant.

What Covenant was that ?—The Covenant of Works.

What is it called besides ?—The Law.

What does the Law give a picture of before-hand ?—The Gospel.

To whom then does the Law lead us ?—To Christ.

Tell me again in what part of the Bible the Law is contained ?—In the Old Testament.

How does the Old Testament lead us to Christ ?—By prophesying of Him.

How besides ?—By its sacrifices, which are a type or likeness of the one sacrifice of Christ.

How besides ?—By teaching us by the moral law what sin is, and thus making us feel the need of the Gospel.

Why is the Old Testament then always read for the First Lesson ?—Because it foreshadows the New Testament.

What does "foreshadows" mean ?—Gives a faint likeness of beforehand.

On what day in the year do we begin to read the Old Testament ?—On January 2nd.

Is it read straight through ?—Yes, excepting some few chapters, and excepting also the Book of Psalms.

And how often can it be read through in the year ?—Only once through in the year.

Which of the Prophetical Books is not read in its proper order, but is appointed for the last six weeks of the year ?—The Book of the Prophet Isaiah.

Why is this ?—Because it contains so many prophecies about the coming of Christ that it is fit that it should be read in the season of Advent.

Are there any days in the year for which proper First Lessons are appointed?—Yes, every Sunday, and every Saint's day and Holy-day.

On what Sunday in the year do we begin the Bible at the 1st Chapter of Genesis?—On Septuagesima Sunday.

For what reason?—Among other reasons, to bring before us the types and figures of the great events commemorated in Holy Week and at Eastertide.

Why should the account of the Passover be read on Easter Sunday?—Because the Passover was the yearly feast-day of the Jews in remembrance of their deliverance from Egypt, and was a type of our great feast-day in remembrance of our deliverance from the bondage of Satan.

For what other reason are the first chapters of Genesis suitable to be read on Septuagesima and the following Sundays?—Because they show us from what state of innocence man has fallen, and thus prepare us worthily to sorrow for sin during Lent.

On what Sundays is the prophet Isaiah read?—During Advent and Epiphany.

Why?—Because he tells of our Lord's coming.

Where are the proper First Lessons for Saints' days and Holy-days taken from?—From some chapter in the Old Testament or in the Apocrypha, which is either a type, or a prophecy, or an illustration of the day.

Why is the Apocrypha read?—As the Sixth Article has it, "for example of life and instruction of manners."

How can we find the First Lesson for the day?

—By looking in the Calendar, and finding the day of the month.

How can we find the proper First Lessons for Sundays ?—By looking in the Table of proper Lessons and finding the Sunday.

How can we find the proper Lessons for Holy-days ?—By looking in the next table, called the Table of Lessons proper for Holy-days.

———◇———

Lesson XI.—The Te Deum.

What follows the First Lesson?—The Te Deum.

What is the Te Deum ?—A Canticle or Hymn of Praise.

How is it repeated ?—Like the Venite, and all the Canticles, it may be either sung, or chanted, or said in alternate verses, by the Minister and People.

Why does a Canticle follow each Lesson ?—Because after having heard God's Word, it is fitting that we should praise and glorify God for the message we have received from it, and the good tidings contained in it.

In what posture do we repeat the Te Deum ? —Standing, because we are praising.

At what time was it written ?—About the 4th century.

For how many years, then, has the Te Deum been used in the Church ? —For nearly 1,500 years.

What may the Te Deum be called ?—A creed turned into a Hymn of Praise.

Why?—Because it contains nearly all the articles of the Creed, and in it we praise God for them.

How is the Te Deum divided?—Into three parts.

What does the first part contain?—Praise to the Holy Trinity; it extends to the end of the 13th verse.

Where does the second part begin?—At the words, "Thou art the King of Glory, O Christ."

What does the second part consist of?—Of praise to God the Son.

Where does the third part begin?—At the 20th verse, "We therefore pray Thee, help Thy servants."

What does the third part contain?—Prayer to God the Son.

Read the Latin words at the head of the hymn.—"Te Deum Laudamus."

What do they mean?—Thee, as God, we praise.

Read the first verse.—"We praise Thee, O God: we acknowledge Thee to be the Lord."

What do you understand by the expression, "the Lord"?—The Lord Jehovah, Who was revealed to Moses, as "I Am That I Am."

What, then, is the meaning of the first verse? —We praise Thee, as God, we acknowledge Thee to be the Lord who revealed Himself to Israel as the Lord Jehovah.

Read the second verse.—"All the earth doth worship Thee, the Father everlasting."

Where is the first half of this verse taken from?—From the 66th Psalm.

For what purpose was the earth and everything

in it made by God ?—That they might glorify and worship God.

When we come to church to worship God, what are we fulfilling ?—One of the chief purposes for which God made us—viz., to worship Him.

What name do we give to God in this second verse ?—The Father everlasting.

Is this title given to God the Son also ?—Yes, in Isaiah ix., "Unto us a Child is born, unto us a Son is given, and He shall be called . . . . the everlasting Father."

Read the next four verses.—"To Thee all Angels cry aloud : the Heavens, and all the Powers therein. To Thee Cherubin, and Seraphin, continually do cry, Holy, Holy, Holy, Lord God of Sabaoth ; Heaven and earth are full of the Majesty of Thy glory."

Of whose praise do we now begin to speak ?—Of that of the angels ; we raise our thoughts from those who praise God on earth, to those who praise Him in Heaven.

What do you understand by " the heavens" ?—Not only the sun and moon, of which we are told that "the heavens declare the glory of God, and the firmament showeth His handiwork" (Psalm xix. 1), but the highest Heavens, where God dwells.

Who are " the powers " in Heaven ?—Different orders of angels.

Who are the " Cherubin" and the " Seraphin "?—Angels.

Where do we read of the Cherubin ?—They were placed at the gate of the Garden of Eden to keep it ; Ezekiel saw them under the likeness of four living creatures; and St. John saw them under the same likeness standing round about the throne.

Who saw the Seraphin?—The prophet Isaiah saw them in a vision, standing above the throne of God, each having six wings.

And what did Isaiah hear the Seraphin cry?—"Holy, Holy, Holy, is the Lord of Hosts."

And what was the song of the Cherubin recorded by St. John?—"Holy, Holy, Holy, Lord God Almighty."

Therefore what do we say in the Te Deum?—"To Thee Cherubin and Seraphin continually do cry, Holy, Holy, Holy, Lord God of Sabaoth."

How do we know that they do it "continually"?—Because St. John says, "They rest not day and night." Rev. iv. 8.

Whom do they acknowledge in this threefold "Holy"?—The Blessed Trinity, "Holy" Father, "Holy" Son, "Holy" Spirit.

What does "Sabaoth" mean?—Hosts or armies.

Is the word Sabaoth ever used in the Bible?—Yes, in the 5th chapter of St. James, God is called the Lord of Sabaoth.

What do we declare that Heaven and earth are full of?—The Majesty of God's glory.

What does "majesty" mean?—Grandeur and splendour.

Read the seventh verse.—"The glorious company of the Apostles praise Thee."

What does "company" really mean here?—Band, or choir.

Read the eighth verse.—"The goodly fellowship of the Prophets praise Thee."

What is a fellowship ?—A society.

Who are the Prophets ?—Those men who in their writings testified of Christ's coming.

How do they praise God ?—They praise Him now in Paradise, as their writings praise Him on earth.

Read the ninth verse.—" The noble army of Martyrs praise Thee."

Who are the Martyrs ?—Those who died for Christ's sake.

What is the literal meaning of the word in the original, here translated " noble " ?—White-robed.

In what manner are the Martyrs " white-robed " ?—St. John says that they are " clothed in white robes with palms in their hands, having washed their robes and made them white in the Blood of the Lamb." Rev. vii. 9, 14.

Read the tenth verse.—" The Holy Church throughout all the world doth acknowledge Thee."

What do we call " the Holy Church throughout all the world " in the Creed ?—The Holy Catholic Church.

What is meant by the Church ?—" A congregation of faithful men," as the Nineteenth Article states it, " in which the pure word of God is preached, and the sacraments be duly ministered, according to Christ's ordinance, in all those things that of necessity are requisite to the same."

Who is it that the Holy Catholic Church acknowledges ?—The Blessed Trinity.

When does it acknowledge the Blessed Trinity ?—First when it baptizes into the new name revealed by Jesus Christ, " into the name of the Father, and of the Son, and of the Holy Ghost."

And when besides ?—Every time it sings the Te Deum, the Creeds, or the Doxology, or in any words gives glory to the Trinity.

What do the next three verses express ?—The object that the Angels, the Apostles, the Prophets, the Martyrs, and the Holy Catholic Church praise and acknowledge.

What is this ?—The Blessed Trinity.

Read the verses—

" The Father, of an infinite Majesty;

" Thine honourable, true, and only Son ;

" Also the Holy Ghost, the Comforter."

In what words do we honour God the Father? —We say that He is " of an infinite Majesty," or that His Majesty is infinite.

What is " infinite " ?—Without bounds or limits.

What do we say of God's Son ?—That He is the honourable, true, and only Son.

What does " honourable " mean ?—Worthy of all honour, " that all men should honour the Son, even as they honour the Father." John v. 23.

Who gave the name of " Comforter " to the Holy Ghost ?—Our Lord, " When the Comforter is come, whom I will send unto you from the Father." John xv. 26.

We have now finished the first part of the " Te Deum," what did you tell me it contains ?—Praise to the Holy Trinity.

What does the second part contain ?—Praise to God the Son.

Read the fourteenth and fifteenth verses.

" Thou art the King of Glory, O Christ.

" Thou art the everlasting Son of the Father."

Where is Christ called the King of Glory ?—In the 24th Psalm, "Lift up your heads, O ye gates, and ye be lift up, ye everlasting doors, and the King of Glory shall come in."

What do you understand by the title " everlasting Son " ?—That the Son has been with the Father from the beginning, from everlasting.

Where are we told so ?—In the prophecy of His birth at Bethlehem, " Out of thee shall He come forth unto me that is to be ruler in Israel; Whose goings forth have been from of old, and from everlasting."   Micah v. 2.

And where besides ?—In the first chapter of St. John. " In the beginning was the Word, and the Word was with God."

Read the next verse.—" When Thou tookest upon Thee to deliver man, Thou didst not abhor the Virgin's womb."

For what do we praise the Son in this verse ? —For His Incarnation.

How did He "take upon Him" to deliver man ? —Of His own will, " Lo, I come to do Thy will, O God."   Heb. x. 7.

From what did He come to deliver man?—From his bondage to sin and death.

What does " abhor " mean ?—Hate, or despise.

How did our Lord show that He" did not abhor the Virgin's womb " ?—By condescending to be born of a lowly virgin.

Read the seventeenth verse.—" When Thou hadst overcome the sharpness of death, Thou didst open the Kingdom of Heaven to all believers."

For what do we praise God the Son here ?—For His Death, His Resurrection, and Ascension.

What is the sharpness of death ?—The sting of death.

And what is that sting ?—"The sting of death is sin." 1 Cor. xv. 55.

How did He overcome this sting ?—By conquering sin and Satan.

What do you understand by "the Kingdom of Heaven" ?—His Kingdom of Glory.

To whom has He opened the gate ?—To all believers.

How has He done so ?—By going in first to prepare a place for them.

Read the next verse.—"Thou sittest at the right hand of God, in the glory of the Father."

Where are we told this ?—St. Mark says that, "He was received up into heaven, and sat on the right hand of God" (xvi. 19) ; and St. Stephen "saw the Glory of God, and Jesus standing on the right hand of God." Acts vii. 55.

Read the nineteenth verse.—"We believe that Thou shalt come to be our Judge."

What reason have we for believing this ?—Because the Father hath committed all judgment unto the Son (John v. 23) ; and because at His Ascension the angels assured His disciples "that this same Jesus shall so come in like manner as ye have seen Him go into heaven." Acts i. 11.

In this second part of the "Te Deum," for what articles of the Creed do we praise God ?—For

"Jesus Christ His only Son our Lord, who was conceived by the Holy Ghost, born of the Virgin Mary; suffered under Pontius Pilate; was crucified, dead, and buried; the third day He rose again from the dead, He ascended into Heaven, and sitteth on the right hand of God the Father Almighty, from thence He shall come to judge the quick and the dead."

What does the last part of the Te Deum contain?—Prayer to God the Son.

Read the twentieth verse.—"We therefore pray Thee, help Thy servants, whom Thou hast redeemed with Thy precious blood."

What does "therefore" mean?—For this reason; because we believe that He will come to be our judge.

On what ground do we plead for His help?—That He has redeemed us with His precious blood.

What does "redeemed" mean?—Bought back.

What does "precious" mean?—Something of very great price. 1 Peter i. 18, 19.

Read the twenty-first verse.—"Make them to be numbered with Thy Saints in glory everlasting."

What is it to be numbered with God's saints?—To be counted amongst them, to be "partakers of the inheritance of the Saints in light." Col. i. 12.

When do we pray to be numbered among His Saints?—In the day when they shall enter "everlasting glory."

Read the next two verses.—"O Lord, save Thy people, and bless Thine heritage. Govern them, and lift them up for ever."

Where do these verses come from ?—From the last verse of the 28th Psalm.

What is a " heritage " ?—An inheritance.

What is our Lord's heritage or inheritance ?—His Church, the children whom God has given Him. Heb. ii. 13.

What do we ask Him to do for His people ?—To save them, bless them, govern or feed them, and lift them up for ever.

What is the real meaning of " lift them up " ?—Help them.

Read the next two verses.—" Day by day we magnify Thee ; and we worship Thy Name ever world without end."

What is it to " magnify " our Lord ?—To make great by speaking of His greatness.

How often shall we magnify, and worship His Name ?—Every day, and " world without end." Psalm cxlv. 2.

Read the twenty-sixth verse.—" Vouchsafe, O Lord, to keep us this day without sin."

What does " vouchsafe " mean ?—Be so gracious.

Who made this prayer before ?—David, " Keep Thy servant also from presumptuous sins." Ps. xix. 13.

Read the next two verses.—" O Lord, have mercy upon us ; have mercy upon us. O Lord, let Thy mercy lighten upon us, as our trust is in Thee."

What does " mercy " mean ?—Pity.

Why do we ask three times for mercy ?—Because our need of it is so great.

What do you understand by the words "lighten

upon us " ?—Descend upon us from above; as we are told the Dove "lighted" upon our Lord after His baptism.

Read the last verse.—"O Lord, in Thee have I trusted; let me never be confounded."

What does "confounded" mean ?—Confused, or put to shame.

Are we ever assured that those who trust in God shall not be confounded ? — Yes: "Our fathers trusted in Thee, . . . and Thou didst deliver them ; . . . they trusted in Thee, and were not confounded." Psalm xxii. 4, 5.

Lesson XII.—The Benedicite.

Is there any Canticle that may be used after the First Lesson instead of the Te Deum ?—Yes, the Benedicite.

What is the other name for the Benedicite ?— The Song of the Three Children.

Where is it found ?—In the Apocrypha.

Who were the Three Children ?—The three who were cast into the burning fiery furnace by Nebuchadnezzar.

Why ?—Because they would not break God's commandments, and worship the golden image.

When is it said in the Apocrypha that they sang this hymn ?—When they were walking in the midst of the fire.

May the Benedicite be used any day instead of the Te Deum ?—Yes, but it is more fitted for times of humiliation, as Lent and Advent.

Why?—Because it is not the highest kind of praise. It does not praise God for all the great things He has done for us as the Te Deum does, but only calls on all His works to praise Him.

For what Sundays besides is it very suitable?—For the 21st Sunday after Trinity, when the account of the young men being cast into the furnace is read in the First Lesson.

And for what other?—For Septuagesima Sunday, when the account of the creation of all God's works, who in the Benedicite are called upon to praise Him, is read.

Read the title of the Canticle.—"Benedicite, omnia opera."

What do these words mean?—They are the first words of the Canticle in Latin, and mean "Bless ye, all works."

Read the first verse.—"O all ye works of the Lord, bless ye the Lord : praise Him, and magnify Him for ever."

What is the difference between this first verse and all the other verses?—The first verse is a summary of the whole. All God's works are called upon to praise Him. In the other verses each separate work is called upon in turn.

What is the meaning of "magnify Him"?—Make great by speaking of His greatness.

Which of God's works is first called upon to praise Him?—The highest of all, the angels of the Lord.

After the angels, which works are next called upon?—All the things that He has created that do not live.

What are these?—The heavens, the waters

F

that be above the firmament, the powers of the Lord, sun and moon, stars of heaven, showers and dew, winds of God, fire and heat, winter and summer, dews and frosts, frost and cold, ice and snow, nights and days, light and darkness, lightnings and clouds, the earth, mountains, and hills, the green things upon the earth, wells, and seas, and floods.

What is meant by the "heavens" and the "firmament"?—The sky that we see over our heads.

What are the "powers of the Lord"?—Those wonderful, unseen powers that He has placed around us, such as gravity, the power that keeps all the planets circling in order round the sun; electricity, the power which we use to send messages with lightning speed to the ends of the earth; and many others.

How can these created things which have "no speech nor language" bless and praise the Lord? —They praise Him by fulfilling His law: "He hath given them a law which shall not be broken." Psalm cxlviii. 6.

After these inanimate works of the Lord, who are next called upon to bless, and praise, and magnify Him for ever?—His living but unreasoning works, in the order in which they were created.

What are they?—Whales, and all that move in the waters, fowls of the air, beasts, and cattle.

After these, which of God's works are next called upon?—Those whom He has endowed with both life and reason, the children of men.

Why is their praise higher than the praise of

the former works of the Lord ?—Because they can praise with the understanding.

And why is it also not so high ?—Because man is fallen. He alone of all God's works cannot perfectly fulfil the purpose of his creation.

After all men in general, which in particular are called upon ?—His chosen people Israel.

Who are His chosen people now?—The Church.

And next ?—The priests of the Lord.

—And after the priests of the Lord ?—The servants of the Lord.

Who are they ?—They were the Levites in the Jewish Church; in the Christian Church they are the deacons, the choir, and all who serve in the Church under the priests.

Who next ?—The spirits and souls of the righteous.

Where are they ?—Resting in hope in Paradise.

Who next ?—Holy and humble men of heart.

Why is the praise of the holy and humble always acceptable to God ?—Because they praise Him with their lives as well as with their lips.

Who are the last that are called upon to bless and praise and magnify the Lord ?—Ananias, Azarias, and Misael.

Who were they ?—The Three Children, the authors of the hymn.

What names do we generally give them ?—Shadrach, Meshach, and Abed-nego. The first were their Jewish names. The latter were the Chaldean names given them when they were in captivity in Babylon.

Which of the Psalms is very much like the

Benedicite, because it calls on God's works to praise Him ?—The 148th.

How does the Benedicite end ? — With the Gloria Patri.

LESSON XIII.—THE SECOND LESSON.

What follows the Te Deum, or the Benedicite ? —The Second Lesson.

Read the first part of the rubric.—"Then shall be read in like manner the Second Lesson, taken out of the New Testament."

What is meant by " in like manner " ?—In the same manner as the First Lesson.

What manner was that ?—It was to be read distinctly, and with an audible voice.

What does that mean ?—Clearly, and with a voice that can be heard.

What is the meaning of the word "Lesson" ? —Reading.

Where is the Second Lesson always taken from ?—From the New Testament.

What does the word " Testament" mean ?— Covenant, or agreement.

Why is the second part of the Bible called the New Testament ?—Because it contains the new covenant.

What covenant is that ?—The covenant of grace.

With whom does God enter into this covenant ?—With all of us.

When ?—When we are baptized and made Christians.

What does God do for us on His side ?—Makes us members of Christ, His children, and heirs of the kingdom of heaven.

What do we promise on our side ?—To renounce sin, to believe the faith, and to keep God's commandments.

Why is this covenant called the Covenant of Grace ?—Because it is of God's favour, not of our merits, that we are admitted into it, because it is by His help alone that we can keep our part of it.

And what part of the Bible contains this covenant ?—The New Testament.

And why is part of the New Testament read for the Second Lesson ?—Because in the First Lesson we heard the Gospel promised, in the Second we hear the promise fulfilled ; in the Old Testament the Gospel was foreshadowed, in the New the shadow is realized.

How is the New Testament divided ?—Into the Gospels, the Acts of the Apostles, the Epistles, and the Book of Revelation.

What do the Gospels contain ?—The good news of the coming and the death, the rising again to life, and the ascension of the promised Saviour.

What does the Book of the Acts of the Apostles contain ? — The history of the foundation and spread of Christ's Church.

What are the Epistles ?—Letters written by different Apostles to the Churches they had founded, to the Bishops Timothy and Titus, and to private people.

What does the Book of Revelation contain? —The vision seen by St. John the Divine, when he was in the island of Patmos.

If the different books of the Bible then were written by different men, how is it that the Bible is the Word of God?——Because all these men were inspired, that is, the Holy Spirit breathed into them and directed them what to write: " All Scripture is given by inspiration of God." 2 Tim. iii. 16. " Holy men of God spake as they were moved by the Holy Ghost." 2 Peter i. 21.

In what manner then ought we to listen to the lessons read to us in church?——With the greatest reverence and the deepest attention, because it is the voice of God Himself speaking to us.

How often in the year is the New Testament read through?——Twice in the year.

Where do you find the Second Lesson for the day?——In the Calendar, opposite the day of the month.

Are there proper Second Lessons for Sundays? —Only for a few, for Septuagesima, Palm Sunday, Easter-Day, First Sunday after Easter, Whit-Sunday and Trinity Sunday.

Where do you find these?——In the Table of Proper Lessons, the same Table that contains the proper First Lessons for Sundays.

For what other days are there proper Second Lessons?——For most of the Saints' Days and Holy Days.

Where do you find them?——In the Table of Lessons proper for Holy Days.

For what reason are proper Second Lessons chosen ? — Because, on particular Sundays, on Saints' Days, and Holy Days, it is fitting that we should hear about the events which are connected with the day.

———•○•———

LESSON XIV.—THE BENEDICTUS.

After the Second Lesson what follows ?—Another Canticle or Hymn of Praise.

Why does a Hymn of Praise always follow the reading of a Lesson ?—That we may sing praises to God in thanksgiving for the good news we have just heard.

Where do we find an example of this ?—In the second chapter of St. Luke. After the angel had told the good news of the birth of a Saviour to the shepherds, immediately a multitude of the heavenly host sang a hymn of praise to God.

What Canticle is to be said or sung after the Second Lesson ?—The Benedictus.

Read the Rubric· before the Benedictus.— "Then shall be read in like manner the Second Lesson, taken out of the New Testament. And after that, the Hymn following; except when that shall happen to be read in the chapter for the day, or for the Gospel on St. John Baptist's day."

On what day in the year does this Hymn " happen to be read in the chapter for the day " ? —On March 25.

What is the meaning of the word Benedictus ?—It means "blessed," and is the first word of the hymn in Latin.

What is the other name for this hymn ?—The Song of Zacharias.

Where is it found ?—In the first chapter of St. Luke.

On what occasion did Zacharias sing it ?—At the circumcision of his son, St. John the Baptist.

Read the first verse.—"Blessed be the Lord God of Israel, for He hath visited and redeemed His people."

What was the subject of Zacharias' Song of Praise ?—The coming of the Saviour.

What does he bless God for in the first verse ?—That He had visited and redeemed His people.

What is to "visit" ?—To come and see in order to help.

On what other great occasion had God visited His people Israel ?—When they were in Egypt.

And when He said to Moses, "I have surely visited you, and seen that which is done to you" (Exod. iii. 16), what did He say He was come to do ?—To deliver them from bondage.

What does "redeem" mean ?—To buy back, as from slavery.

And of what was the Egyptian slavery a type ?—Of the harder slavery to Satan.

And of what was their redemption from Egypt a type ?—Of the greater redemption brought by Christ, when God "visited and redeemed His people."

Read the second verse.—"And hath raised up

a mighty salvation for us in the house of His servant David."

What does a " mighty salvation" mean ?—A mighty Saviour or saving power.

How was it that this was raised up " in the house of His servant David "?—Because the Saviour was born of the house or family of David : " I will raise unto David a righteous branch, and a King shall reign and prosper." Jeremiah xxiii. 5.

Read the next two verses.—" As He spake by the mouth of His holy Prophets, which have been since the world began ; that we should be saved from our enemies, and from the hands of all that hate us."

Which was the first of these holy Prophets ? —Enoch. See Jude 14.

And which the last ?—Malachi.

What was it that God spake by their mouth ? —The promise that He would raise up a mighty Saviour for us, to save us from our enemies; and from the hands of all that hate us.

Who are these enemies that hate us ?—The devil and his angels, the world, the flesh, and bad men.

Read the next two verses.—" To perform the mercy promised to our forefathers, and to remember His holy Covenant ; to perform the oath which He sware to our forefather Abraham, that He would give us."

Who are the " forefathers" mentioned here ?— Adam, Abraham, Isaac, Jacob, and others.

What was the mercy promised to them ?— That the seed of the woman should bruise the serpent's head. Gen. iii. 15.

What was the holy Covenant that He remembered ?—The Covenant He made with Abraham, "In thee shall all families of the earth be blessed." Gen. xii. 3.

What oath did He sware to Abraham ?—"By Myself have I sworn, saith the Lord, in thy seed shall all nations of the earth be blessed." Gen. xxii. 16, 18. "Because He could swear by no greater, he sware by Himself." Heb. vi. 13.

"That He would give unto us." What do you understand by this ?—That He would grant unto us ; and the next two verses tell us what He promised to grant unto us.

Read them.—"That we being delivered out of the hand of our enemies, might serve Him without fear ; in holiness and righteousness before Him, all the days of our life."

For what purpose has God redeemed us out of the hand of our enemies ?—That we may serve Him all the days of our life.

With what sort of service ?—A service of love.

What sort of service is the service of a slave ? —A service of fear.

But what is it that casts out fear ?—Perfect love casteth out fear. 1 John iv. 18.

And with what sort of lives are we to honour Him who has redeemed us ?—Holy and righteous lives.

Read the next two verses.—"And thou, Child, shalt be called the Prophet of the Highest : for thou shalt go before the face of the Lord to prepare his ways ; to give knowledge of salvation unto His people for the remission of their sins."

Whom does Zacharias now address, when he

says, "And thou, Child"?—His son, John the Baptist.

What does he say his son shall be called?—The Prophet of the Highest.

What is a prophet?—A teacher. One who gives a message from God.

Who is the Highest?—The coming Saviour.

In what manner did John the Baptist "go before the face of the Lord to prepare His ways"?—He preached repentance, and thus prepared people's hearts for a Saviour.

What does giving "knowledge of salvation" mean?—He made known to people the expected salvation.

What was this salvation?—"The remission, or forgiveness, of their sins" through Christ.

Read the last verses.—"Through the tender mercy of our God, whereby the dayspring from on high hath visited us; to give light to them that sit in darkness, and in the shadow of death, and to guide our feet into the way of peace."

What claim have we to this salvation, this remission of our sins?—None. It is given us "through the tender mercy of our God."

What does "whereby" mean?—By which, through which.

What is the "dayspring"?—The dawn, the first herald of the sun.

Who is represented by this emblem of "the dayspring"?—Our Lord Jesus Christ, who is called "the bright and morning star" (Rev. xxii. 16), and "the Sun of Righteousness" (Malachi iv. 2).

What does the dayspring come to do?—"To

give light to them that sit in darkness, and in the shadow of death."

Who were those who, before Christ's coming, sat "in darkness and in the shadow of death"?—The Gentiles; "the people which sat in darkness saw great light; and to them which sat in the region and shadow of death light is sprung up." Matt. iv. 16.

For what else does "the dayspring visit us"?—To guide our feet into the way of peace.

What is the way of peace?—The way of true wisdom, of which it is said, "her ways are ways of pleasantness, and all her paths are peace." Prov. iii. 17.

How do we end the Benedictus?—With the Gloria Patri.

LESSON XV.—THE JUBILATE.

On those days when the Benedictus is not to be used, what may be sung or said after the Second Lesson instead?—The Jubilate.

What is the Jubilate?—The 100th Psalm.

Read the words at the head of it.—Jubilate Deo.

What do they mean?—Be joyful in God.

In what way do the verses in the Jubilate answer each other?—The first and third contain invitations to rejoice and praise God in His temple. The second and fourth answer, and give reasons for our joy.

Read the first verse.—" O be joyful in the Lord,

all ye lands ; serve the Lord with gladness, and come before His presence with a song."

When do we come before His presence ?—When we come to church.

And what is the highest sort of worship we offer there ?—Praise.

Read the second verse.—" Be ye sure that the Lord He is God : it is He that hath made us, and not we ourselves; we are His people and the sheep of His pasture."

What reasons are given in this verse for being joyful in the Lord ?—Because we are sure that He is the true God, that He is our Creator, our Ruler, and our Shepherd.

Who were His people and the sheep of His pasture when this Psalm was written ?—The children of Israel.

Who are His people now ?—Members of His Church.

What is God's pasture ?—The Church; the fold where He feeds His sheep.

Read the third verse.—" O go your way into His gates with thanksgiving, and into His courts with praise ; be thankful unto Him, and speak good of His name."

Why is God's House spoken of here as having gates and courts ?—Because the Jewish temple had many gates and courts.

What do you understand here by " His Name"? —The titles and attributes by which He has revealed Himself to us.

In this third verse also, to which part of God's worship are we invited ?—To praise.

Read the fourth verse.—" For the Lord is

gracious, His mercy is everlasting; and His truth endureth from generation to generation."

What reasons again are given in the fourth verse for praising God?—That He is gracious, merciful, true, and unchanging.

What does " endureth " mean?—Lasteth.

What is " from generation to generation "?—From living men down to their children, and again to their children, and so on.

When these Psalms were sung by Jewish saints of old times, could they add to them the Gloria Patri as we do?—No; for God had revealed Himself to them only by His name Jehovah, they did not know His name of Father, Son, and Holy Ghost.

But may Christians add the Gloria Patri to them?—Yes; for our Lord has revealed that great Name to us, and no hymn of praise can be perfect that does not ascribe glory to the Blessed Trinity.

———

LESSON XVI.—THE APOSTLES' CREED.

What does the first part of the Morning Service consist of?—Of a Service of Praise.

How does the Service of Praise end?—With a confession of our faith.

What is this confession of faith called?—The Apostles' Creed.

What does the word " creed " mean?—It comes from the Latin word *credo*, " I believe."

Read the rubric.—" Then shall be sung or

said the Apostles' Creed by the Minister and the people, standing; except only such days as the Creed of Saint Athanasius is appointed to be read."

Why may the Creed be sung as well as said?—Because it is in some sense a Hymn of Praise.

By whom is the Creed to be repeated?—By both Minister and people with one voice.

Why should each person in the congregation repeat it?—Because each is professing his own faith, the faith he promised at his baptism to believe. Romans x. 10.

In what posture are Minister and people to be while repeating the Creed?—Standing.

Why?—To express that they stand firm in the faith, and also to do honour to the faith they profess.

Why is it customary in many churches also to turn to the east when repeating the Creed?—Because the sun which gives us light rises in the east, and the Lord is our Sun of Righteousness. The early Christians always followed this custom, because they expected our Lord at his second coming to appear in the east.

Why do we bow at the name of Jesus when we repeat the Creed?—Because such a mark of reverence is prescribed by the 18th Canon of the Church.

When is the Apostles' Creed not repeated in the Morning Service?—On those days when the Creed of St. Athanasius is appointed to be read instead.

What days are these?—On the six festivals of Christmas, Epiphany, Easter, Ascension-Day,

THE LITANY.

Find the Litany in your Prayer-books. What is the meaning of the word Litany ?—A supplication.

Read the rubric.—"Here followeth the Litany, or General Supplication, to be sung or said after Morning Prayer upon Sundays, Wednesdays, and Fridays, and at other times when it shall be commanded by the ordinary."

Why are Sundays, Wednesdays, and Fridays chosen as the days for the Litany to be used ?—Sundays, because it is fitting to use more services on the day especially set apart for worship, and Wednesdays and Fridays, because they are less joyful than other days of the week, and therefore suited to this solemn supplication.

Why is Wednesday one of the less joyful days of the week ?—Because it is said to have been the day of our Lord's betrayal.

And Friday ?—Friday is a fast-day, and the saddest day of the week, because on Friday our Lord was crucified.

Who is the ordinary ?—The Bishop.

Can you think of any other days in the year when it is fitting to use the Litany ?—Any fast-day, especially the three Rogation-days.

Which are the three Rogation-days ? — The Monday, Tuesday, and Wednesday before Ascension Day.

What does Rogation mean ?—It means the same as Litany, viz. Supplication.

For what special purpose were the Rogation-days set apart as days of supplication ?—For a blessing on the fruits of the earth.

As Litany means supplication, what is the posture of Minister and People while they are saying it ?—All kneeling.

What other direction does the rubric give about the Litany, besides the days on which it is to be used ?—It directs that it may be either said or sung.

What else may we notice about the Litany?—That it is very full of responses for the people.

Into how many parts may the Litany be divided?—Into four parts.

What are they ?—1. The Invocations. 2. The Deprecations. 3. The Intercessions. 4. The Supplications.

———◇———

PART I.—THE INVOCATIONS.

What is an invocation ?—Calling upon any one by his name.

Whom do we invoke in the Litany ?—The Blessed Trinity.

Read the first invocation.—" O God the Father, of heaven : have mercy upon us miserable sinners."

What do you understand by the words " of heaven " ?—In heaven.

Is it right to say " the Father of heaven " without separating the words ?—No, we do not mean that God is the Father of heaven, but that He is the Father, and that He dwells in heaven.

Read the second invocation.—"O God the Son,

Redeemer of the world: have mercy upon us miserable sinners."

What do you understand by the words " Redeemer of the world " ?—That by His precious blood, God the Son has bought back the whole world from the slavery and bondage of Satan, the prince of this world, and paid the price that we deserved to pay for our sins.

Read the third invocation.—" O God the Holy Ghost, proceeding from the Father and the Son: have mercy upon us miserable sinners."

Where besides here are we taught in the Prayer-book that God the Holy Ghost proceedeth from the Father and the Son ?—In the Nicene Creed, " I believe in the Holy Ghost; who proceedeth from the Father and the Son."

Where in the Bible are we taught this doctrine? —In our Saviour's words, " when the Comforter shall come, whom I will send unto you from the Father." John xv. 26.

Having called upon each Person of the Blessed Trinity in turn, whom do we lastly invoke ?— The Holy Trinity as one God.

Read the last invocation.—" O Holy, Blessed, and Glorious Trinity, three Persons and one God; have mercy upon us miserable sinners."

What do we call the doctrine that teaches us that there are three persons, and but one God? —The doctrine of the Trinity in Unity.

To whom was this doctrine first plainly revealed ?—To the Apostles, when our Lord told them to go and baptize all nations into the Name of the Father, and of the Son, and of the Holy Ghost.

For what purpose do we invoke each Person of the Godhead, and then the Holy Trinity?—To ask them to "have mercy upon us."

What do we call ourselves?—"Miserable sinners."

What does "miserable" mean? — Needing pity.

Why are sinners so needful of pity? — Because they cannot help themselves, they can only throw themselves on the mercy of God.

PART II.—THE DEPRECATIONS.

What part of the Litany follows the Invocations?—The Deprecations.

What are the "Deprecations"?—Prayers to avert evils; prayers that some evils may not happen to us.

To whom are all the deprecations addressed?—To God the Son.

Read the first.—"Remember not, Lord, our offences, nor the offences of our forefathers; neither take Thou vengeance of our sins: spare us, good Lord, spare Thy people, whom Thou hast redeemed with Thy most precious blood, and be not angry with us for ever. Spare us, Good Lord."

How do you know, when we are calling upon the "Lord" here, that we are addressing God the Son?—Because we say, "whom Thou hast redeemed with Thy most precious blood."

What are " offences " ?—Sins.

What do we mean when we ask the Lord not to " remember " our offences ?—We ask Him to blot them out of His book, so that when He comes to judge us they may not be mentioned against us.

What else do we mean ?—That He will not remember them and send us any punishment for them in this world.

Why do we also ask Him not to remember the sins " of our forefathers " ?—Because we are taught in the Second Commandment that God will " visit the sins of the fathers upon the children."

Does this mean that children will suffer eternally for their fathers' sins ?—No. " The soul that sinneth, it shall die. The son shall not bear the iniquity of the father, neither shall the father bear the iniquity of the son." Ezek. xviii. 20.

What, then, does it mean ?—That children suffer in this world for their fathers' sins.

Therefore what do we ask for when we pray " remember not the offences of our forefathers" ? —Turn from us the sufferings that are due to us through our forefathers' sins.

What besides do we pray God not to do ?— " Neither take Thou vengeance of our sins."

Have we any reason to hope that we shall be heard when we cry " Spare us, good Lord " ?— Yes ; we may say spare Thy " people," for we hope He will spare us because we belong to Him.

And what still greater reason do we plead ?— That He has redeemed us with His precious blood; He has bought us with so great a price that we may trust He will not cast us off again.

Have we any promise that if we repent, He will not " be angry with us for ever " ?—" He will not always be chiding; neither keepeth He His anger for ever." Ps. ciii. 9 (Prayer-book version).

Read the next Deprecation.—" From all evil and mischief; from sin, from the crafts and assaults of the devil; from Thy wrath, and from everlasting damnation, Good Lord, deliver us."

What is "mischief" ?—Anything that does us harm.

What are the "crafts" of the devil ?—His cunning and deceit.

What are his "assaults" ?—His attacks.

How can we guard against his crafts and assaults ?—By being " sober and watchful; for he goeth about as a roaring lion, seeking whom he may devour." 1 Peter v. 8.

What is "everlasting damnation" ?—The eternal punishment of the wicked in hell, who "shall be punished with everlasting destruction from the presence of the Lord." 2 Thess. i. 9.

Read the next.—" From all blindness of heart; from pride, vain-glory, and hypocrisy; from envy, hatred, and malice, and all uncharitableness, Good Lord, deliver us."

What is "blindness of heart" ?—Being unable to see our own faults, or to see the right way to God.

What is "pride" ?—A high opinion of ourselves.

And " vain-glory " ?—Liking others to think much of us.

And " hypocrisy " ?—Pretending to be better than we are.

What commandment forbids " envy, hatred, malice, and all uncharitableness " ?—The sixth.

What do all these bad feelings against our neighbour cause us to do ?—" Envy " makes us angry because he has something that we have not ; " hatred " makes us his enemy ; " malice " makes us wish to hurt him ; and " uncharitableness " causes us to think and speak evil of him.

What are the next sins and evils from which we ask God to deliver us ?—" From fornication, and all other deadly sin ; and from all the deceits of the world, the flesh, and the devil, Good Lord, deliver us."

What sort of sins do we here pray against ?—Sins of the flesh.

Why are they called deadly ?—Because they are so hateful in the sight of a pure and holy God, and because they kill the soul.

Who are the three great enemies we have to fight against ?—The world, the flesh, and the devil.

What are their " deceits " ?—The ways by which they try to deceive us and make us think that sins are not sins.

Having prayed to be delivered from all these ghostly dangers, what do we next ask for ?—For deliverance from some bodily dangers.

What are they ?—" From lightning and tempest ; from plague, pestilence, and famine ; from battle and murder ; and from sudden death, Good Lord, deliver us."

What evils are caused by "lightning and tempest"?—They destroy the fruits of the earth, wreck many ships, and sometimes kill men.

What are "plague and pestilence"?—Grievous sicknesses.

And "famine"?—A want of food through the land.

What do you mean by "battle"?—Going to war, and having such fighting that many are killed.

What is meant by "sudden death"?—A death that comes without warning and at a time when we are not prepared.

Can you remember any instances of these outward evils being sent by God as punishments?—"Lightning and tempest" were sent upon Egypt when Pharaoh refused to let the children of Israel go. "The Lord sent thunder and hail, and the fire ran along upon the ground; and the hail smote every herb of the field, and brake every tree of the field." Exodus ix. 23, 25.

And "plague and pestilence"?—When David offended the Lord by numbering the people, "the Lord sent a pestilence upon Israel, and there died of the people seventy thousand men." 2 Sam. xxiv. 15. And fourteen thousand men who followed Korah and despised Moses died of the plague. Num. xvi. 49.

And "famine"?—A famine which lasted three years and six months was sent upon Israel in the time of Elijah, to punish Ahab for his sins. 1 Kings xvii. 1.

What evils do we next pray against?—Evils

hurtful first to the Government, secondly to the Church, and thirdly to ourselves.

Read the words:—"From all sedition, privy conspiracy, and rebellion; from all false doctrine, heresy, and schism; from hardness of heart, and contempt of Thy Word and Commandment, Good Lord, deliver us."

What is "sedition"?—Unlawful talking and agitating against the Government.

What is likely to follow sedition?—"Privy conspiracy"; that is, private plots against it.

And what does privy conspiracy often break out into?—"Rebellion"; that is, open disobedience to our rulers.

Why is it our duty to obey our Government and our rulers?—Because God has commanded us to do so. "Let every soul be subject unto the higher powers. For there is no power but of God: the powers that be are ordained of God. Whosoever therefore resisteth the power resisteth the ordinance of God." Rom. xiii. 1, 2. "Submit yourselves to every ordinance of man for the Lord's sake: whether it be to the king as supreme, or unto governors, as unto them that are sent by him." 1 Peter ii. 13, 14.

What are the evils hurtful to the Church from which we ask God to deliver us?—"All false doctrine, heresy, and schism."

What is "false doctrine"?—Teaching which does not agree with the teaching of the Bible and the Church. Jude 3.

What is "heresy"?—Wilful choosing, and perseverance in, false doctrine after being warned against it. "They will not endure sound doctrine." 2 Tim. iv. 3.

What do false doctrine and heresy lead to ?— To schism.

What is " schism " ?—Dividing and separating from the Church, and forming sects which choose their own doctrines, and follow teachers who have never had authority given them to guide the flock. " After their own lusts (wishes) shall they heap to themselves teachers having itching ears, and they shall turn away their ears from the truth." 2 Tim. iv. 3, 4.

What are the last things we ask our Lord to deliver us from ?—Hardness of heart and contempt of His word and commandment.

What is " hardness of heart " ?—Carelessness and indifference,—not feeling or minding when we do wrong.

What does this lead to ?—To contempt of God's teaching and laws, and despising His reproofs. " I have called, and ye refused; I have stretched out My hand, and no man regarded.; but ye have set at nought all My counsel, and would none of My reproof." Prov. i. 24, 25.

How do we end the deprecations ?—By pleading what Christ has done for us, as a reason for hoping that He will grant our prayers.

Read the first part of our pleadings :—"By the mystery of Thy Holy Incarnation; by Thy Holy Nativity and Circumcision; by Thy Baptism, Fasting, and Temptation, good Lord, deliver us."

What is meant by the word "by" here ?— For the sake of.

What does "mystery" mean ?—Something we cannot understand.

What is Christ's " Incarnation " ?—His being made flesh.

Why is this a mystery ?—Because we cannot understand how God could be made man.

What is His " Nativity " ?—His birth.

And His " Circumcision " ?—His being circumcised, according to the law, on the eighth day.

Where was His " Baptism " ?—In the river Jordan.

And His " Fasting " ?—In the wilderness for forty days.

What was His " Temptation " ?—The great conflict He had with Satan, when Satan was conquered and forced to flee.

Why do we plead His Incarnation and Birth as reasons for His hearing and delivering us ?—Because by taking our flesh and being born in our nature, He partook of all our weakness and infirmities.

Why do we plead His " Circumcision " ?—Because by it He " became obedient to the law for man."

And His "Baptism" ?—Because, by being baptized He " fulfilled all righteousness," and " sanctified water to the mystical washing away of sin."

Why do we plead His " Fasting " ?—Because He " fasted for our sakes," to show us how to " subdue the flesh to the spirit."

And His " Temptation " ?—Because, being " in all points tempted like as we are, yet without sin," He can be " touched with the feeling of our infirmities."   Heb. iv. 15. And " in that He Himself hath suffered, being tempted, He is able to succour them that are tempted."   Heb. ii. 18.

Read the remainder of our Pleadings.—" By thine Agony and Bloody Sweat ; by Thy Cross and Passion ; by Thy precious Death and Burial ; by Thy glorious Resurrection and Ascension ; and by the coming of the Holy Ghost, Good Lord, deliver us."

What was His " Agony and Bloody Sweat " ? —The great suffering of Christ in the Garden of Gethsemane, when " His sweat was as it were great drops of blood falling down to the ground."

What was His " Cross and Passion " ?—The dreadful means of His death, and His sufferings upon it.

What is meant by the word " Passion " here ? —Suffering.

What was His " precious Death and Burial " ? —His giving up His spirit into the hands of His Father at the ninth hour of that awful day, and the laying of His body in the sepulchre by the pious hands of Joseph and Nicodemus.

Why is His Death called " precious " ?— Because it is of such infinite worth to us, because it paid the whole sum due for our sins.

What was His " glorious Resurrection and Ascension " ?—His rising to life again with His glorified body on the morning of the third day, and His ascending up to Heaven in the sight of His disciples forty days after, to enter in triumph into Heaven, and to sit down on the right hand of God.

What was the " coming of the Holy Ghost " ?— The promised descent of the Comforter upon the Apostles, ten days after our Lord had left them.

L

Why do we plead Christ's Agony and Bloody Sweat?—Because He suffered both in body and spirit under the weight of the sins of the whole world.

And His Cross and Passion?—Because He was "made a curse for us, as it is written, cursed is every one that hangeth on a tree" (Gal. iii. 13), and suffered in our stead.

Why do we plead His death and burial?—Because "through death He destroyed him that had the power of death, that is the devil" (Heb. ii. 14), and through His burial He sanctified the grave, through which we must all pass.

And His glorious Resurrection and Ascension?—Because by His Resurrection He bruised the serpent's head, and "became the first fruits of them that slept" (1 Cor. xv. 20); and by His Ascension He entered into the presence of God to plead His sacrifice for us (Heb. ix. 12).

And why do we plead the coming of the Holy Ghost?—Because Christ thus remembered His promise not to leave us comfortless, but sent Him to teach and sanctify us.

Having in the Deprecations asked God the Son to deliver us from all hurtful things, and pleaded the great things He has done for us, as reasons why we hope He will hear us, how do we end?—By numbering over the particular times when we most stand in need of help and deliverance.

Read the words.—"In all time of our tribulation; in all time of our wealth; in the hour of death, and in the day of judgment, Good Lord, deliver us."

What is "tribulation"?—Any trouble.

Why do we need deliverance then?—Lest we should lose our faith, and think God has forsaken us.

Why need we never despair when we are in tribulation?—Because our Lord Himself said, "In the world ye shall have tribulation; but be of good cheer, I have overcome the world" (John xvi. 33); and we know that "we must through much tribulation enter into the Kingdom of God" (Acts xiv. 22).

What is "wealth"?—Happiness and well-doing.

Why do we need deliverance then?—Lest we should be exalted and forget God.

Why do we ask for deliverance in "the hour of death"?—Because that is the hour of our greatest need, when "the flesh and the heart faileth," and none can help us but Christ alone.

And in "the day of judgment"?—That in that dreadful day we "may be accounted worthy to escape all those things that shall come to pass, and to stand before the Son of Man." Luke xxi. 36.

PART III.—THE INTERCESSIONS.

What is the next part of the Litany after the Deprecations?—The Intercessions.

What are Intercessions?—Prayers for others.

How do the people respond in the Intercessions?—By the words, "We beseech Thee to hear us, God Lord."

Whom are we still addressing?—God the Son.

For whom do we first intercede ?—For the Church.

Read the words.—"We sinners do beseech Thee to hear us, O Lord God ; and that it may please Thee to rule and govern Thy Holy Church universal in the right way ; we beseech Thee to hear us, Good Lord."

What do we begin by confessing ourselves to be ?—Sinners.

Is it allowed to sinners to intercede for others ?—Yes ; St. Paul says, "I exhort therefore, that, first of all, supplications, prayers, intercessions, and giving of thanks be made for all men."

What is the "Holy Church Universal" ?—The Holy Catholic Church.

What do we pray for the Holy Catholic Church ?—That its Lord may rule and govern it in the right way.

What does that mean ?—That it may be kept free from false doctrines and wrong practices.

For whom are the next three clauses of intercession ?—For our Queen.

Read them all three.—"That it may please Thee to keep and strengthen in the true worshipping of Thee, in righteousness and holiness of life, Thy servant Victoria, our most gracious Queen and Governor. That it may please Thee to rule her heart in Thy faith, fear, and love, and that she may evermore have affiance in Thee, and ever seek Thy honour and glory ; that it may please Thee to be her defender and keeper, giving her the victory over all her enemies. We beseech thee to hear us, Good Lord."

What is the first thing we ask for the Queen?
—That she may worship God aright.

And the next?—That her life may be righteous and holy.

Why should the life of a sovereign be especially just and righteous?—Because "he that
ruleth over men must be just, ruling in the fear
of God." 2 Sam. xxiii. 3.

From whom does she receive authority to
reign?—From God, "By me kings reign"
(Prov. viii. 15), and therefore she is His "servant," although our "Queen and Governor."

What is the third thing we ask for her?—
That God will rule her heart in His faith and fear
and love.

Why do we ask for these three in this order?
—Because the "fear" of the Lord is the beginning of wisdom, and "love" is the perfection of
it, while "faith" must come first of all as the
foundation of both.

And the next?—That she may evermore have
affiance in God.

What is "affiance"?—Trust.

And in all that she does for her country and
people, what do we pray she may seek for first?
—The honour and glory of God.

What is the last thing we pray for her?—
Help in all outward perils, and victory over her
enemies.

For whom do we next intercede?—For the
Royal Family. "That it may please Thee to bless
and preserve Albert Edward, Prince of Wales,
the Princess of Wales, and all the Royal Family;
We beseech Thee to hear us, Good Lord."

Why amongst all the Royal Family do we especially pray for the Prince of Wales?—Because
he is heir to the throne, and will be our next
sovereign if he live.

For whom do we pray next?—For the three
orders of the Clergy.

Read the words.—"That it may please Thee
to illuminate all Bishops, Priests, and Deacons
with true knowledge and understanding of Thy
word; and that both by their preaching and
living they may set it forth and show it accordingly; We beseech Thee to hear us Good Lord."

What is to "illuminate"?—To shed light upon.

Why do the Clergy especially need a true
knowledge and understanding of God's Word?
—Because they have to explain and teach it to
the people.

How ought they to set forth God's Word?—
By their preaching and their living.

How can they "show it accordingly" by their
living?—By making their lives "accord" (or
agree) with the Word they preach.

Read the next intercession.—"That it may
please Thee to endue the Lords of the Council,
and all the Nobility, with grace, wisdom, and
understanding; We beseech Thee to hear us,
Good Lord."

What does "endue" mean?—Clothe.

Who are the "Lords of the Council"?—The
ministers of State who govern the country.

And the "nobility"?—The House of Lords,
who help to make our laws.

Why do they need "grace, wisdom, and
understanding"? — To prevent them from

making mistakes, from guiding the country wrong, and making bad laws.

Read the next intercession.—"That it may please Thee to bless and keep the magistrates, giving them grace to execute justice, and to maintain truth; We beseech Thee to hear us, good Lord."

Who are the "magistrates"?—All judges and justices who administer the laws when they are made, and see that we carry them out and obey them.

Why do they need grace?—That they may always be fair and just, and boldly maintain (or uphold) what is right and true.

Having now prayed for all who are put in authority over us, for whom do we next intercede?—For all God's people. "That it may please Thee to bless and keep all Thy people; We beseech Thee to hear us, good Lord."

For whom next?—For all nations.

Read the words.—"That it may please Thee to give all nations unity, peace, and concord; We beseech Thee to hear us, good Lord."

What are all "nations"?—The different countries of the world.

What is "unity"?—Being joined together as one. "Behold how good and joyful a thing it is, brethren, to dwell together in unity." Psalm cxxxiii. 1 (Prayer-book version).

What is "peace"?—Freedom from war.

And "concord"?—Agreement.

For what sort of blessings do we pray in the next two clauses?—For inward and spiritual blessings.

Read the first of these.—" That it may please Thee to give us an heart to love and dread Thee, and diligently to live after Thy commandments ; We beseech Thee to hear us, good Lord."

When we ask for a " heart to love and dread " God, what duty are we asking for grace to perform ? — Our duty towards God, which is to believe in Him, to fear Him, and to love Him.

What is meant by walking " after " His commandments ?—According to them.

In what other place is the word " after " used in this sense ?—" O Lord, deal not with us after our sins."

How is this " diligent " walking after God's commandments described in the Book of Deuteronomy ?—" And these words which I command thee this day shall be in thy heart : and thou shalt teach them diligently to thy children, and shalt talk of them when thou sittest in thy house, and when thou walkest by the way, and when thou liest down, and when thou risest up " (chap. vi. 6, 7).

Read the next.—" That it may please Thee to give to all Thy people increase of grace, to hear meekly thy Word, and to receive it with pure affection, and to bring forth the fruits of the Spirit ; We beseech thee to hear us, good Lord."

What is " increase " of grace ?—More and more grace.

Why is more and more needed ?—Because though the first grace is given at baptism, it is not sufficient to carry us through our journey unless we are " daily renewed by the Holy Spirit."

What is it to hear the Word with " meekness " ?—With a willingness to be taught.

What is it to receive it with pure " affection " ? —With the deepest love for it.

And what is it to bring forth the fruits of the spirit ?—To show by our good works that the Word sown in our hearts has not been wasted.

What part of the parable of the Sower should we try to have fulfilled in us ?—The part which describes the seed sown on good ground. " That on the good ground are they, which in an honest and good heart, having heard the Word, keep it, and bring forth fruit with patience." Luke viii. 15.

For whom do we next pray ?—For the wanderers from Christ's fold.

Read the words.—" That it may please Thee to bring into the way of truth all such as have erred and are deceived; We beseech Thee to hear us, good Lord."

Who are these ?—Those who have wandered from the way of truth, and having followed false teachers or false books, have let themselves be deceived, till they " put darkness for light, and light for darkness." Isaiah v. 20.

What do we ask the Lord to do for them ?— To show to them " the light of His truth, to the intent that they may return into the way of righteousness."

Read the next intercession.—" That it may please Thee to strengthen such as do stand, and to comfort and help the weak-hearted; and to raise up them that fall ; and finally to beat down

Satan under our feet; We beseech Thee to hear us, good Lord."

Why do those who "stand" need strengthening?—Because we are warned by St. Paul, "Let him who thinketh he standeth, take heed lest he fall." 1 Cor. x. 12.

Who are the "weak-hearted"?—Those who fear for themselves, who run with trembling the race that is set before them, and who are ready to faint and be "discouraged because of the way." Numb. xxi. 4.

What do these need?—Comfort and help.

What is meant by "those that fall"?—Those that fall into some sin.

How will God "raise them up"?—By restoring them to His favour, on their repentance, and setting their feet again upon a rock. Psalm xl. 2.

For whom, then, do we pray in this intercession?—For all the Baptized; for all Christians must be in one of the three spiritual states recognized by our Church, either standing, or weak-hearted, or fallen.

When will Satan be at last beaten down under our feet?—When we "have fought the good fight, and finished our course." 2 Tim. iv. 7.

For whom do we next intercede?—For those in trouble. "That it may please Thee to succour, help, and comfort all that are in danger, necessity, and tribulation; We beseech Thee to hear us, good Lord."

What do we ask for those in "danger"?—Succour. "In the day of salvation have I succoured thee." 2 Cor. vi. 2.

And for those in "necessity" ?—Help. "Blessed is he that hath the God of Jacob for his help." Psalm cxlvi. 4 (Prayer-book version).

And for those in "tribulation" ?—Comfort. "Who comforteth us in all our tribulation." 2 Cor. i. 4.

For whom do we next pray ?—For those at that moment in positions of peculiar danger.

Read the words.—"That it may please Thee to preserve all that travel by land or by water, all women labouring of child, all sick persons, and young children; and to show Thy pity upon all prisoners and captives; We beseech Thee to hear us, good Lord."

What do we ask for those who "travel by land" ?—That the Lord will preserve them from all dangers, and bring them safe to their journey's end, as those whom "He led forth by the right way, that they might go to the city where they dwelt." Psalm cvii. 7 (Prayer-book version).

And for those who "travel by water" ?— That the Lord will preserve them through storm and tempest, and "bring them unto the haven where they would be." Psalm cvii. 30 (Prayer-book version).

And for "sick persons" ?—That the Lord will "comfort them when they lie sick upon their bed, and make all their bed in their sickness." Psalm xli. 3 (Prayer-book version).

Why do we intercede for "young children" ? —Because they are so weak and tender.

Does our Lord take peculiar care of young children ?—Yes, for He said, "Suffer the little children to come unto Me." Mark x. 14.

Who are " prisoners " ?—Those put in prison for some crime.

And " captives " ?—Those taken in war.

What do we ask the Lord to do for them ?— To show His pity on them. " Let the sorrowful sighing of the prisoners come before Thee." Psalm lxxix. 12 (Prayer-book version).

In what way ?—By granting freedom to the latter, and to the former repentance and restoration to their place in the world.

Read the next intercession.—" That it may please Thee to defend, and provide for, the fatherless children, and widows, and all that are desolate and oppressed ; We beseech Thee to hear us, good Lord."

Are the fatherless children and widows the peculiar care of God ?—Yes. " He is a Father of the fatherless." Psalm lxviii. 5 (Prayer-book version). And He has said, " Leave thy fatherless children. I will preserve them alive; and let thy widows trust in Me." Jer. xlix. 11.

What do we ask Him to do for them ?—To defend and provide for them.

Against whom may they need defence ? — Against any who would oppress them because they have no earthly protector.

Who are the " desolate " for whom we also ask God's defence and care ?—Those who have no friends.

And the "oppressed " ?—Those who are hardly treated by some more powerful than they.

For whom do we next pray ?—For those who are not included in any of the former intercessions. " That it may please Thee to have mercy upon all men ; We beseech Thee to hear us, good Lord.''

Read the next intercession.—" That it may please Thee to forgive our enemies, persecutors, and slanderers, and to turn their hearts ; We beseech Thee to hear us, good Lord.''

Who are our " enemies " ?—Those who wish us harm.

And " persecutors " ?—Those who persevere in doing us harm.

And " slanderers " ?—Those who speak evil against us falsely.

Why should we pray for them ?—Because our Lord bids us " pray for them which despitefully use you and persecute you." Matt. v. 44.

Whose example are we following in so doing ? —Our Lord's Himself (Luke xxiii. 34). And St. Stephen's (Acts vii. 60), and the Apostles' (1 Cor. iv. 12, 13).

For what do we next pray ?—That the Lord will give us the fruits of the earth in their season.

Read the words.—" That it may please Thee to bless and preserve to our use the kindly fruits of the earth, so as in due time we may enjoy them ; We beseech Thee to hear us, good Lord.''

In what way does God bless the fruits of the earth ?—By making the seed we sow spring up and grow.

And from what do we ask Him to preserve them ? — From all blight, or too much rain or drought or anything which would prevent the fruits coming to perfection.

What do you understand by "fruits"?—
Everything that grows on the earth for man's use.

What does "kindly" fruit mean?—Each fruit
after its kind or sort. Gen. i. 12.

What does enjoying them "in due time"
mean?—In their proper season, when they are
ripe, and the time of their harvest is come.

Read the last intercession.—"That it may
please Thee to give us true repentance; to forgive us all our sins, negligences, and ignorances;
and to endue us with the grace of Thy holy
Spirit, to amend our lives according to Thy holy
Word; We beseech Thee to hear us, good Lord."

Why must we pray for repentance?—Because
it is a gift of God. We cannot repent of our
own efforts. Acts viii. 22.

What sort of repentance may be called
"true"?—A repentance that leads to amendment.

What promise have we that God will forgive
our sins?—"If we confess our sins, God is faithful and just to forgive us our sins." 1 John i. 9.

What are "negligences"?—Sins of omission;
that is, duties that we have neglected, and left
undone.

What are "ignorances"?—Sins that we committed in our ignorance, not knowing better.

If "repentance" is not "true" unless it leads
to amendement, what do we need after forgiveness
of our sins?—The grace of God's Holy Spirit.

For what purpose?—That we may amend our
lives.

How shall we know how to amend our lives?
—By examining ourselves by "God's holy
Word."

How are the Intercessions finished ?—By addressing God the Son, to Whom we have been praying, by three of His titles, and then by repeating the Lesser Litany.

By what title do we first address our Lord ?—Son of God, we beseech Thee to hear us.

And next ?—O Lamb of God, which takest away the sins of the world ; grant us Thy peace. O Lamb of God, which takest away the sins of the world, have mercy upon us.

By whom are we first taught to call Him " Lamb of God " ?—By St. John the Baptist. " Behold the Lamb of God." John i. 29.

Why is our Lord called the Lamb of God ?—Because as a lamb, He was sacrificed for us, and on Him we feed at our Passover feast.

What peace do we ask Him to grant us ?—His peace, the peace He left with His disciples ; " Peace I leave with you, My peace I give unto you." John xiv. 27.

What is the third title by which we address our Lord ?—Christ, the anointed, Prophet, Priest, and King; " O Christ, hear us."

What follows this threefold address to God the Son ?—The Lesser Litany.

What is that ?—The call upon the Three Persons of the Blessed Trinity to have mercy upon us.

Read the words.—" Lord, have mercy upon us ; Christ, have mercy upon us ; Lord, have mercy upon us."

Whom do we address the first time we cry " Lord, have mercy upon us " ?—God the Father.

And who is " Christ " ?—God the Son.

And again, whom do we address as "Lord"?—God the Holy Ghost.

What does "have mercy" mean?—Pity, and spare.

In what other Services is this Lesser Litany used?—In the Morning and Evening Services.

----◦◦----

PART IV.—THE SUPPLICATIONS.

What does the fourth and last part of the Litany consist of?—Of the Supplications.

With what do they begin?—With the Lord's Prayer.

Read the rubric.—"Then shall the Priest, and the people with him, say the Lord's Prayer." "Our Father, which art in heaven, Hallowed be Thy Name. Thy Kingdom come. Thy will be done in earth, As it is in heaven. Give us this day our daily bread. And forgive us our trespasses, As we forgive them that trespass against us. And lead us not into temptation; But deliver us from evil. Amen."

Why do we use the Lord's Prayer in the Litany?—Because no Service can be perfect without obeying our Lord's command, "When ye pray, say, Our Father." Luke xi. 2.

Is there anything to be remarked about the Lord's Prayer as used in the Litany?—The Doxology is left out.

Why so?—Because the Litany is a Service of Prayer, and not of Praise.

What follows the Lord's Prayer?—A versicle and response.

What is a " versicle " ?—A short verse.

And a " response " ?—An answer.

Read them.—" O Lord, deal not with us after our sins. Neither reward us after our iniquities."

What does " after " mean ?—According to.

What are " iniquities " ?—Evil deeds.

What does " deal not with us " mean ?—Do not treat us.

What then do we pray in this versicle and response ?—Do not treat us according as our sins deserve, nor give us the proper wages of our evil deeds.

Why does the Priest next say " Let us pray " ? —To remind the people to keep their attention fixed, and to pray with their hearts, although they are no longer to join with their voices as much as before.

Read the address of the prayer following.— " O God, merciful Father, that despiseth not the sighing of a contrite heart, nor the desire of such as be sorrowful."

What grounds of hope do we here put forth that God will hear our prayer ?—First, that He is our " Merciful Father."

And secondly ?—That in the words of David, " a broken and a contrite heart He does not despise." Ps. li. 17 (Prayer-book version).

What is a " contrite " heart ? A heart worn down with sorrow for sin.

And what is the " desire " that he does not despise ?—The wish to do better of those who sorrow for sin, or the wish for deliverance for those who are in trouble.

Read the prayer.—" Mercifully assist our

M

prayers that we make before Thee, in all our troubles and adversities whensoever they oppress us; and graciously hear us, that those evils which the craft and subtlety of the devil or man worketh against us, be brought to nought; and by the providence of Thy goodness they may be dispersed."

Why do we need God to "assist" us in our prayer? — Because "we know not what we should pray for as we ought." Rom. viii. 26.

In what time especially may we as children of God go to our merciful Father?—"In all our troubles and adversities whensoever they oppress us."

What are "adversities"?—Things that go against us.

What is it to "oppress" us?—Weigh us down.

What especial evils do we ask may be brought to nought?—Those "which the craft and subtlety of the devil or man worketh against us."

What is "craft"?—Cunning.

And "subtlety"?—Artfulness.

When does man follow the example of the devil?—When he tries by cunning and artfulness to make others sin.

What do we ask God to do about the evils which the devil or man try to bring upon us?— To bring them to nought and disperse them.

What does "bringing them to nought" mean?—Making them come to nothing.

And "dispersing" them?—Scattering them to the winds.

What do you understand by "the providence

of thy goodness "?—The care and kindness by which God provides help for those who trust in Him. "The Lord is on my side, I will not fear what man can do unto me." Ps. cxvii. 6.

Read the rest of the Prayer.—"That we Thy servants being hurt by no persecutions, may evermore give thanks unto Thee in Thy holy Church, through Jesus Christ our Lord. *Amen.*"

What are "persecutions"?—The harm that Satan and bad men try to work against good men.

What is it that prevents persecution hurting the servants of God?—The protection of their Heavenly Father.

And when safe from persecution, how will God's servants remember Him who has saved them?—By "evermore giving thanks unto Him."

Why do we add "in Thy holy Church"?—Because that is the place of safety where Christians are always near their Defender,—the fold in which Satan can do them no lasting harm.

Do the congregation answer "Amen" at the end of this prayer?—No; they say a longer response.

Read it.—"O Lord, arise, help us, and deliver us for Thy Name's sake."

Where is this response taken from?—From Psalm xliv. 26.

What do we mean when we say, "for Thy Name's sake"?—Help us, and deliver for the sake of that name which Thou didst proclaim to be "the Lord God, merciful and gracious, long-suffering, and abundant in goodness and truth."

M 2

Exod. xxxiv. 6. Let Thy mercy and goodness still be shown for our help.

Read the versicle of the Priest that follows.—"O God, we have heard with our ears, and our fathers have declared unto us the noble works that thou didst in their days, and in the old time before them."

Where do these words come from ?—From Psalm xliv. 1.

What noble works of God had the Israelites heard from their fathers ?—The deliverance from Egypt and bondage, and the destroying of all their enemies before their face when they entered Canaan.

What besides ?—The wonderful victories of the Judges, and of David and their other Kings.

What besides ?—The redemption from Babylon and the restoration to their own land.

And what noble works of God have we Christians heard of from our fathers?—Of the foundation of the Church in our own land not very long after the times of the Apostles ; of the conversion of our heathen forefathers by the preaching of Augustine, of the preservation of the true faith of the Catholic Church in our land from that time down to our own age.

What is the response of the people.—"O Lord, arise, help us, and deliver us for thine honour."

What is the meaning of this response ?—That as God has done these noble works in old times, so we pray that for His own honour He will not forsake us, but will help us as He did our forefathers, and deliver us, too, from our enemies.

What follows this response?—The Gloria Patri, in praise for God's noble works: "Glory be to the Father, and to the Son, and to the Holy Ghost; as it was in the beginning, is now, and ever shall be, world without end. *Amen.*"

After the Gloria Patri, or Doxology, what follows?—Five versicles and responses.

To whom are they all addressed?—To God the Son.

Read the first versicle and response.—"From our enemies defend us, O Christ. Graciously look upon our afflictions."

Who are our enemies?—The world, the flesh, and the devil.

Why have we such confidence in asking Christ's defence from them?—Because He Himself conquered them all.

What are "afflictions"?—Sorrows and troubles.

Why do we believe that He will look upon them with pity?—Because of His deep love and sympathy. "In all their affliction He was afflicted, and the angel of His presence saved them." Isaiah lxiii. 9.

Read the next.—"Pitifully behold the sorrows of our hearts. Mercifully forgive the sins of Thy people."

What verse of the Psalms do these words remind you of?—"Turn Thee unto me, and have mercy upon me, for I am desolate and in misery. Look upon my adversity and misery, and forgive me all my sin." Ps. xxv. 15, 17 (P.-book vers.).

Can you mention any instance of Christ "pitifully beholding the sorrows of the heart"?

—When He saw the widow of Nain, and had compassion on her, and said unto her, "Weep not."—Luke vii. 13.

Read the next.—"Favourably with mercy hear our prayers.   O Son of David, have mercy upon us."

What does "favourably" mean?—With favour, that is, willingness to grant.

Who was it cried, "O Son of David, have mercy upon us"?—The blind men who sat by the wayside as our Lord was near Jericho.

Why does the same cry suit us?—Because we, too, are blind, and do not see our own sins.

Read the next.—"Both now and ever vouchsafe to hear us, O Christ.   Graciously hear us, O Christ; graciously hear us, O Lord Christ."

What does "vouchsafe" mean?—Be so gracious as to.

What promise have we that He *will* graciously hear us?—"And this is the confidence that we have in Him, that if we ask anything according to His will, He heareth us." 1 John v. 14.

Why do we repeat "graciously hear us, O Lord Christ"?—Because we are sinners, and He is of such infinite Majesty, that we feel that it is only with the deepest humility we dare approach.

Read the last versicle and response.—"O Lord, let Thy mercy be shewed upon us.   As we do put our trust in Thee."

Where do these words come from?—From Ps. xxxiii. 21.

What do they express?—That God's mercy will be showed to us just according to the faith and confidence we have in Him : "Trust in the

Lord with all thine heart, and lean not unto thine own understanding. In all thy ways acknowledge Him, and He shall direct thy paths." Prov. iii. 5, 6. " The Lord shall stand by them and save them; He shall deliver them from the ungodly, and shall save them, because they put their trust in Him."—Ps. xxxvii. 41 (Prayerbook version).

Did our Saviour make us any such promise?— Yes. " According to thy faith be it unto thee." Matt. ix. 29.

What follows the versicles?—Another prayer.

What does the Priest say before beginning it? —Let us pray.

Why does he say this?—To remind the people again to give their attention and pray with their hearts, so as to be able to say with sincerity the *Amen* at the end.

Read the first part of the prayer.—"We humbly beseech Thee, O Father, mercifully to look upon our infirmities; and for the glory of Thy Name turn from us all those evils that we most righteously have deserved."

Whom do we address in this prayer?—God the Father.

How do we approach Him?—With humility, " we humbly beseech Thee."

What are " infirmities "?—Weaknesses.

What do we mean when we ask Him to look upon our infirmities " mercifully "?—We ask Him to " remember that we are but dust " (Ps. ciii. 14), and not to be angry with us for our sins, because we are so weak and so easily led into temptation.

What do we acknowledge ?—That we have righteously deserved any evils that may happen to us.

What is "righteously" ?—Justly.

In what Collect do we acknowledge the same ? —In that for Septuagesima, when we are preparing for heaven.

Nevertheless, what do we ask our Heavenly Father to do ?—To turn away these evils from us, although we have deserved them.

Read the rest of the prayer.—"And grant that in all our troubles we may put our whole trust and confidence in Thy mercy, and evermore serve Thee in holiness and pureness of living, to Thy honour and glory; through our only Mediator and Advocate, Jesus Christ, our Lord. *Amen.*"

What do you understand by the words "that in all our troubles we may put our whole trust and confidence in Thy mercy" ?—That if God does send us troubles, we may feel sure that He only sends them in love, and thus learn to trust Him that He will remove them when He sees fit.

What does "mercy" mean ?—Kindness.

And what is having "confidence" in God's mercy ?—Having a faith in it which nothing can shake. And whether the "evils we righteously deserve" are turned from us, or whether we have learnt to bear our "troubles" in trust and confidence, what do we ask that we may do ?— Evermore serve our Father in holiness and pureness of living.

Why do we add "to Thy honour and glory" ?

—Because God is honoured by the good lives of His people, and because, as the power to live a good life comes only from Him, so to Him only belongs the Glory : " Not unto us, O Lord, not unto us, but unto Thy Name give the praise." Ps. cxv. 1 (Prayer-book version).

Through whom do we offer up this prayer ?— Through "our only Mediator and Advocate, Jesus Christ our Lord."

What is a "mediator" ?—One who mediates, or comes between. " There is one Mediator between God and man, the man Christ Jesus." 1 Tim. ii. 5.

And an "advocate" ?—One who pleads or speaks for another : " If any man sin, we have an advocate with the Father, Jesus Christ the righteous." 1 John ii. 1.

How does the Litany end ?—As in the Morning and Evening Services, with the Prayer of St. Chrysostom and the Blessing.

A FEW QUESTIONS ON THE COMMINATION
SERVICE.

Whereabouts in the Prayer-book do you find the Commination Service ?—It is the last service before the Psalms.

What is the meaning of the word Commination ?—Threatening.

What is this Service called besides " A Commination " ?—A " denouncing of God's anger and judgments against sinners."

What besides does the Service contain ?—" Certain Prayers."

On what day is the Commination Service appointed to be read ? — On Ash-Wednesday, the First Day of Lent, and at any other time the Ordinary may appoint.

Who is the Ordinary ?—The Bishop.

In what part of the Morning Service is the Commination to be read ?—After the Litany.

How does it begin ?—With an address from the Priest.

Of what does he speak in this address ?—First, of the godly discipline of the Primitive Church.

What is meant by the Primitive Church ?—The Church in early times, in the times of the Apostles, and a few hundred years after.

What is " discipline " ?—Strict order.

And what were the strict orders of the Church in the beginning of Lent ?—That members of the Church convicted of open sin should be put to open penance.

And what besides ?—They were not admitted to the Holy Communion.

Does St. Paul order any such discipline ?—Yes, in the fifth chapter of his first Epistle to the Corinthians we read, " For I have judged already, as though I were present, concerning him that hath done this deed, in the name of our Lord Jesus Christ, when ye are gathered together, to deliver such an one to Satan for the destruction of the flesh, that the spirit may be saved in the day of the Lord Jesus.　Therefore put away from among yourselves that wicked person."　1 Cor. v. 3, 4, 5, 13.

What does " delivering unto Satan " mean ? —Excommunicating from the Church.

Can you mention two men whom St. Paul himself excommunicated ? — Hymenæus and Alexander.　1 Tim. i. 20.

Why was this godly discipline given up ?—Because during the corruptions of the Church in after-ages, it sank into a mere form of confession, with sprinkling of ashes, on the first day of Lent, for all, whether open offenders or not.

When the Church was cleansed and purified at the Reformation, what was put in the place of this former godly discipline, until it may be restored again ?—The reading in the presence of the congregation of " the general sentences of God's cursing against impenitent sinners."

For what purpose are these sentences to be read ?—That being warned " of the great indignation of God against sinners," we may be "moved to earnest repentance," and flee from the vices to which we acknowledge the curse of God is due.

Where are these sentences taken from?— From the 27th chapter of Deuteronomy.

When were these cursings afterwards uttered? —When the Israelites had entered the Promised Land.

And from what spot were they uttered?— From Mount Ebal.   Joshua viii. 33, 34; Deut. xxvii. 13.

After the Priest has read each curse, what are the people to answer?—Amen.

Do we then go to church on Ash-Wednesday to curse others?—Certainly not.

How do you know we do not?—Because if we did so the Priest would utter the curse as a prayer, and we should mean " So be it " when we said Amen.

But what does the Priest do?—He reads the curse as a fact, not announced by himself, but by God's Word, and we answer " Amen," which means here " So it is," " I believe it is so."

If the Priest were calling down curses on sinners, how would he read the first sentence, for instance?—He would say, " Cursed *be* the man," or " May the man be cursed, that maketh any carved or molten image, to worship it."   And our " Amen " would answer " So be it."

But how does he say the sentence?—He says " Cursed *is* the man," etc., and he only says what God's Word says.   And we agree, and answer " Amen," " So it is."

Can you tell me of any other time when

"Amen" means "So it is," and not "So be it"?—At the end of the Creeds.

Why have I asked you so many questions about this?—Because so many ignorant persons think we go to church on Ash-Wednesday to "curse our neighbours."

Of whom should we think when we hear these curses read?— Principally of ourselves, and of our own danger.

After the reading of these cursings of God against impenitent sinners, how does the service proceed?—With a long and earnest exhortation from the Minister to repent, and turn from our sins, before the day of vengeance overtake us, and throw ourselves at the foot of the Cross, where alone we can obtain forgiveness.

What follows the exhortation?— The fifty-first Psalm (which is deeply penitential), said by the Priest and people on their knees.

And afterwards?— The Lesser Litany, the Lord's Prayer, and four versicles and responses.

What follows the versicles?—Two prayers said by the Minister entreating God's mercy and forgiveness, and another by him and the people together.

How does the Commination Service end?—With the Blessing from the Book of Numbers, chapter vi., verses 24–26.

On what other days, besides Ash-Wednesday, may the prayers of the Commination Service be fitly used?—On any other day, if the Bishop order it.

How many days are there in Lent?—Forty.

To what day does it extend?—To Easter Eve,

which makes forty days, leaving out the six Sundays, which are not fast days.

For what is Lent set apart ?—For a time of fasting and repentance.

Why is the exact time of forty days chosen ?—Because our Lord fasted forty days in the wilderness.   Matt. iv. 2.

And why is it fixed at this part of the Christian year ?—To prepare us for the contemplation of our Lord's Cross and Passion at the close of it.

As repentance is needful every day of our lives, why should a special time be set apart for it ?—Because just as our houses, though cleaned every day, or every week, need a thorough cleaning once a year, so our souls might have many a hidden sin left lurking in them which we have passed over in the hurry of our every-day work, were there not a certain special time set apart every year for searching into our hearts, and bringing these sins out to the light, to be repented of and laid at the foot of the Cross.

Why is fasting ordered by the Church during Lent ?—Because our Lord set us the example, and "for our sakes fasted forty days and forty nights."

Where does our Lord commend fasting ?—Mark ii. 20 : "When the bridegroom shall be taken away from them, then shall they fast in those days."

In what position does our Lord put fasting ?—He counted fasting as one of the three great Christian duties ; viz. Almsgiving, Prayer, and Fasting.   Matt. vi. 18.

Is there any merit in fasting ?—None. There is no merit in any of our works.

What is the use of fasting ?—"That our flesh may be subdued to the spirit." Collect for First Sunday in Lent.

What does that mean ?—That our souls may get the victory over our bodies, and the latter may not stand in the way of our duty.

Is it difficult to get the victory over the flesh ? —Yes, we are naturally so self-indulgent that unless we mortify and deny ourselves we become unfit and unable to take up our cross and follow Christ.

How does fasting help us ?—By making us practise self-denial, a hard lesson which never can be learnt without much practice.

Upon what do the benefits of fasting depend ? —Upon the spirit in which it is done.

What did St. Paul affirm about it ?—"I keep under my body, and bring it into subjection, lest by any means when I have preached to others, I myself should be a castaway." 1 Cor. ix. 27.

Does St. Paul advise us to fast ?—Yes, he recommends us at certain times to give ourselves to fasting and prayer. 1 Cor. vii. 5.

Does David ever speak of fasting ? — Yes, many times. "I humbled my soul with fasting." Psalm xxxv. 13 (Prayer-book version). "I wept, and chastened my soul with fasting." Psalm lxix. 10 (Prayer-book version).

Can you number up some of the good people in the Old Testament of whom we are told that they fasted ?—Moses (Exod. xxxiv. 28), Samuel (1 Sam. vii. 5, 6), David (2 Sam. xii. 16), Elijah

(1 Kings xix. 8), Jehoshaphat (2 Chron. xx. 3), Ezra (Ezra viii. 21), Nehemiah (Neh. i. 4), and even the heathen king of Nineveh (Jonah iii. 6, 7).

And in the New Testament ? — Our Lord Himself (Matt. iv. 2), John the Baptist and his disciples (Mark ii. 18), St. Peter (Acts x. 9), Cornelius (Acts x. 30), Anna (Luke ii. 37), the heads of the Church at Antioch (Acts xiii. 2, 3), St. Paul and St. Barnabas (Acts xiv. 23 ; 2 Cor. vi. 5).

If all these saints were accustomed to fast, and if our Lord Himself set us the example of doing so, what may we be sure about fasting ?—That it is a duty a Christian cannot altogether neglect without injury to his soul's health.

THE END.

WYMAN AND SONS, PRINTERS, GREAT QUEEN STREET, LONDON, W.C.

PUBLICATIONS

OF THE

Society for Promoting Christian Knowledge.

*Most of these Works may be had in ornamental bindings,
with gilt edges, at a small extra charge.*

[1. 12. 75.]   [Fcap. 8vo.

Price.
s. d.

Ellen North's Crumbs.
By ANNA H. DRURY, Author of "Richard Rowe's Parcel," &c. With three full-page illustrations on toned paper. Fcap. 8vo .... *cloth boards*   1   6

First Rector of Burgstead, The.
A Tale of the Saxon Church. By the Rev. E. L. CUTTS, B.A., Author of "The Villa of Claudius," "St. Cedd's Cross," &c. With three full-page illustrations on toned paper. Fcap. 8vo .... *cloth boards*   1   6

Fortunes of the Fletchers, The: a Story of Life in Canada and Australia.
By C. H. EDEN, Esq. With three full-page illustrations on toned paper. Crown 8vo .... *cloth boards*   2   6

Gather up the Fragments.
Two full-page woodcuts, on toned paper. Fcap. 8vo *cloth boards*   1   6

Golden Gorse, and Uncle Mark's Snowballs.
By FLORENCE WILFORD. With three illustrations on toned paper. Crown 8vo .... *cloth boards*   1   6

Heroes of the Arctic and their Adventures.
By FREDERICK WHYMPER, Esq., Author of "Travels in Alaska." With Map, eight full-page illustrations and numerous small woodcuts. Crown 8vo ......*cloth boards*   5   0

His Heart's Desire.
With three full-page illustrations on toned paper. Crown 8vo ....*cloth boards*   1   6

Honest Owen and his Blind Sister.
18mo .... *cloth boards*   1   0

In and Out of London; or, The Half-Holidays of a Town Clerk.
By the Rev. W. J. LOFTIE, B.A., F.S.A., Author of "A Century of Bibles," &c. With four full-page illustrations and numerous small engravings. Post 8vo *cloth boards*   2   6

Janetta; or, The Little Maid-of-all-Work.
With three illustrations on toned paper. Crown 8vo *cloth boards*   1   5

King's Namesake, The.
A Tale of Carisbrooke Castle. By CATHERINE MARY PHILLIMORE. With four full-page illustrations on toned paper. Crown 8vo .... *cloth boards*   2   0

Klatsassan, and other Reminiscences of Missionary Life in British Columbia.
By the Rev. R. C. LUNDIN BROWN, M.A. With Map, and three full-page illustrations on toned paper. Post 8vo *cloth boards*   3   0

Ling Bank Cottage: a Tale for Working Girls.
With two illustrations on toned paper. Crown 8vo *cloth boards*   2   0

Price.
s. d.

Lofty Aims and Lowly Efforts: a Tale of Christian Ministry.
With three full-page illustrations on toned paper. Crown 8vo ....*cloth boards* 3 0

Mary: a Tale of Humble Life.
With three illustrations on toned paper. Crown 8vo *cloth boards* 2 0

Meg's Primroses, and other Stories.
By H. M. CHESTER. On toned paper, with four full-page illustrations. Royal 16mo .... *cloth boards* 2 0

Message, The, and other Stories.
With three full-page illustrations on toned paper. Crown 8vo .... *cloth boards* 2 0

Michael Penguyne; or, Fisher Life on the Cornish Coast.
By W. H. G. KINGSTON. With three full-page illustrations on toned paper. Crown 8vo .... *cloth boards* 1 6

Narrative of a Modern Pilgrimage through Palestine on Horseback, and with Tents.
By Rev. ALFRED CHARLES SMITH, M.A. Numerous illustrations and four coloured plates. Crown 8vo *cloth boards* 5 0

New Stories on Old Subjects.
By C. E. BOWEN, Author of "Stories on My Duty towards God and My Neighbour," &c. With four full-page illustrations on toned paper. Crown 8vo *cloth boards* 3 0

Panelled House, The: a Chronicle of Two Sisters' Lives.
By M. BRAMSTON. With three illustrations on toned paper. Crown 8vo .... *cloth boards* 3 6

Parables of Life.
By Author of "Earth's Many Voices." Royal 16mo, on toned paper, with seven illustrations, *cloth brds, gilt edges* 2 0

Postmaster of Prenslau, The, and other Tales.
From the German. With two page woodcuts, on toned paper. Crown 8vo............................... *cloth boards* 1 6

Stories of Success, as illustrated by the Lives of Humble Men who have made themselves Great.
By JAMES F. COBB, Esq., Author of "Silent Jim." With four illustrations on toned paper. Crown 8vo *cloth boards* 3 0

Stranger than Fiction.
A Story of Mission Life. By the Rev. J. J. HALCOMBE, M.A. With eight full-page illustrations on toned paper. Post 8vo ....*cloth boards* 2 6

The Children of Seeligsberg: a Tale of the Lake of Lucerne.
By the Author of "Madeleine's Forgiveness," "The Cathedral Organist"...... .... 1 6

Prices
s. d.

The Story of the Old Plank, and other Wonder Tales.
Translated from the Dutch. By the Rev. JOHN WIDDI-
COMBE, late Master of St. Andrew's Grammar School,
Bloemfontein. 18mo .... *cloth boards* 1 o

**Thousand Years, A; or, The Missionary Centres of
the Middle Ages.**
By the Rev. JOHN WYSE. On toned paper, with four
illustrations. Crown 8vo .... *cloth boards* 2 6

Uncle Tom's Stories; or, Buzzes from Insect Land.
On toned paper, with four full-page illustrations. Royal
16mo .... *cloth boards* 1 6

Village Beech-Tree, The; or, Work and Trust.
With four full-page illustrations on toned paper. Crown
8vo .... *cloth boards* 2 6

**Wreath of Mallow, The, and other Stories more or
less true.**
By Mrs. JEROME MERCIER. With three page wood-
cuts, on toned paper. Crown 8vo .... *cloth boards* 2 o

Year in the Country, A: a Tale of the Seasons.
On toned paper. Royal 16mo ....*cloth boards* 1 6

New Series of 3s. 6d. Books.

*Post 8vo, with Coloured Frontispiece and Title, Four Full-page
Woodcuts, and numerous small Engravings.*

**A Cruise on the Bosphorus, and in the Marmora and Ægean
Seas.**
By the Rev. G. FYLER TOWNSEND, M.A., Author of "The
Sea Kings," "Siege of Colchester," &c.

Away on the Moorland: a Highland Tale.
By A. C. CHAMBERS, Author of "Robin the Bold," &c.

Julian's Dream. A Story of A.D. 362.
By the Rev. GERALD S. DAVIES, Author of "Gaudentius," &c.

Rosamond Ferrars.
By M. BRAMSTON, Author of "The Panelled House," &c.

The Settlers: a Tale of Virginia.
By W. H. G. KINGSTON, Esq., Author of "The Two Ship-
mates," "Michael Penguyne," &c.

Two Campaigns: a Tale of Old Alsace.
By A. H. ENGELBACH, Esq., Author of "Lionel's Revenge," &c.

Depositories:

77, GREAT QUEEN STREET, LINCOLN'S-INN FIELDS;
4, ROYAL EXCHANGE; 48, PICCADILLY;
AND BY ALL BOOKSELLERS.

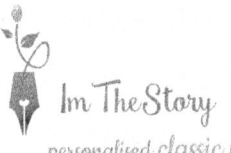

9 781318 694433